"R. T. brilliantly expounds the undiluted biblical truth, beauty and 'scandal' of the Gospel."

— *Lyndon Bowring,*
CEO CARE

"Sobering words you will thank God for."

— *Colin Dye, senior minister*
of Kensington Temple

"This book not only has heart, it has real guts and that's not surprising because it has been written to put guts into us. As I read it, I was heartened, inspired and strengthened in faith. Above all, I came away from this book loving Jesus afresh, passionately committed to serving Him without fear of what anyone may say, but simply to walk in obedience to the Loving Lord."

— *Eric Delve,*
St. Luke's Maidstone

UNASHAMED
TO BEAR
HIS NAME

UNASHAMED TO BEAR HIS NAME

EMBRACING THE STIGMA
OF BEING A CHRISTIAN

R.T. KENDALL

Chosen

a division of Baker Publishing Group
Minneapolis, Minnesota

© 2012 by R. T. Kendall

Published by Chosen Books
11400 Hampshire Avenue South
Bloomington, Minnesota 55438
www.chosenbooks.com

Chosen Books is a division of
Baker Publishing Group, Grand Rapids, Michigan

Printed in the United States of America

Library of Congress Cataloging-in-Publication Data
Kendall, R. T.
    Unashamed to bear His name : embracing the stigma of being a Christian /
R.T. Kendall ; foreword by Ken Costa.
      p. cm.
    ISBN 978-0-8007-9516-0 (pbk. : alk. paper)
    1. Identification (Religion) 2. Christianity. 3. Christian life. I. Title
BV4509.5.K375 2012
248.4—dc23   2011036910

Cover design by Dan Pitts

12   13   14   15   16   17   18   7   6   5   4   3   2   1

Grace always has about it the scent of scandal.
                                    — *Philip Yancey*

To Ricky and Sharon

CONTENTS

Foreword by Dr. Michael Youssef   13
Special Recommendation by Ken Costa   15
Special Recommendation by the Rev. Dr. Clive Calver   17
Preface   21
Introduction   23

1   Personal Background   27
2   The Gospel   39
3   The Most Important Question   49
4   The Offense in the Old Testament   61
5   Embracing the Shame of the Name   75
6   Name-Calling   87
7   The Unnecessary Scandal   97
8   Out on a Limb   109
9   The Reason the Jews Missed Their Messiah   125
10   The Stigma of No Vindication   135
11   The Stigma of Suspicion   145
12   The Stigma of the Holy Spirit   157
13   Manifestations of the Holy Spirit   167
14   Embarrassing Truths   179
15   Outside the Camp   191

FOREWORD

DR. MICHAEL YOUSSEF

Many of us never thought we would see the day when a true Christian anywhere in the world would be called, in the least, "controversial," or at the most, someone who needed to be silenced or even exterminated, as is the case in extreme militant anti-Christian societies.

But that should not surprise us. The Christian faith began as a stigma both to Jews, who did not want a Messiah who hung on a cross, and to the Romans, who detested anyone who taught that there is only one God and only one way to that God.

To be sure, we have had two thousand years of Christian influence, but the world has conveniently forgotten that all of Western civilization had only one solid rock foundation, namely, the Christ of Christianity.

It appears that we are entering into a period that resembles first-century Rome. This ought to take us back to the basics. Back to the Beatitudes, in which Jesus heaps blessings not on "the rich and famous" but on those who are scandalized by being His disciples.

R. T. Kendall, in this masterful work, *Unashamed to Bear His Name*, reminds us of our true heritage as believers in and disciples of Jesus the Messiah. R. T.'s life work of refusing to hide behind the prestigious walls of Westminster Chapel, choosing instead to stand on the streets of London preaching Christ, breathes power into his words.

This is a book that every serious Christian must read, and I daresay every pre-believer should read and be challenged by it. I have no doubt many will be encouraged to take that step of faith into this wonderful and marvelous, scandalous life in Christ.

— *Dr. Michael Youssef*
Senior minister, Church of the Apostles, Atlanta, Georgia
Founder of Leading the Way

SPECIAL RECOMMENDATION

KEN COSTA

Although it was not a physical tattoo, the number 46664 could have been. This was the number the prison authorities in South Africa imposed on Nelson Mandela on Robben Island. For 25 years he carried this stigma in captivity and since then this number has become his imprint worn as a wristband by him and many others, myself included.

The stigma of his imprisonment number is now the reminder of the freedom he fought for.

I was reminded of this when reading R. T.'s compelling and encompassing book.

The connotations of being a marked one are not always pleasant. For Mandela it was imprisonment. But as Saint Paul puts it in the end of the letter to the Galatians, we bear in our bodies the marks of Jesus. What are these Christian tattoo marks?

Are they real?

R. T. gives a magisterial series of answers to these questions. And it is a very contemporary question for everyone—especially those at work. How do we show in the harshness of the workplace that we bear a distinctive Christian imprint?

As always, R. T. writes with conviction. He does not dilute the message. The message of the cross was and always will be a stumbling block. Not everyone will agree with the conclusions he reaches in explaining some of the key issues on the atonement or some of the hotly debated topics. But his views are clearly expressed and left to be weighed by the reader. As ever, gems abound, quarried from the richness of his pastoral experience. Anointing and suffering. Twins?

Christian life can only be experienced in its fullness if we embrace the unavoidable stigma that marks us as followers of Christ. That is his central message, which will come as a healthy antidote to those who believe that painless Christianity is the *menu de jour.*

Every Christian needs to take on the imprint of Christ and learn to live with it every day. This book does not pander to our desire for effortless discipleship. Instead, with straight hard talking he reminds us that it is the biblical Gospel, and nothing else, that is the power of God unto salvation.

So he calls us to embrace the stigma of living for Christ. Not only because it is unavoidable—but because it is the greatest liberation we can ever know. In showing off our tattoo marks we demonstrate to a spiritually hungry society that only a relationship with Christ can truly fulfill our humanity.

— *Ken Costa*
Chairman of Alpha International

SPECIAL RECOMMENDATION
THE REV. DR. CLIVE CALVER

.

I don't know if you are at all like me. If you are, then you'd rather be popular than unpopular. In many of us there is a deep, innate desire simply to be liked.

In order to achieve that objective, we are prepared to make sacrifices. There is usually some give and take regarding integrity, honesty, straightforwardness and intention, all encompassed in this passionate conviction that if people like us, then our lives are going to be much easier and our dreams much more readily fulfilled.

It's this passion for popularity—this commitment to being liked—that has haunted me since I was a child. Like so many of us, I never found it easy to stand on territory where people would want to bring me down, to undermine me or to destroy the things for which I stood.

So I would rather blend into the crowd than take a stand for something different—especially when people might well dislike me for the stand I want to take.

For most of my life, though, God has demanded that I do stand up and stand out. I've always found that when I was most comfortable, God would shift me into a position of being un-comfortable. When I thought I was getting along with people, God would move me on to cause problems in a different com-munity. So it's been strange to want to be liked and often be denied that possibility.

This could very easily sound like a sob story. You can expect the mournful strains of violins any moment now. We all feel sorry for ourselves at times, but it is true that some of us need to be liked more than others do. I've probably always had the desire to stand out from the crowd, but I've never felt very com-fortable doing it. It's one of the detriments of being an introvert with a passion to speak out publicly on issues that concern me, and it practically guarantees that I'll end up near the bottom of the popularity list!

My Jesus was exactly the same. He had many opportunities to be popular. As He walked into the Kidron Valley and went down into the Mount of Olives, he was greeted with choruses of "Hosanna, Hosanna," people shouting not a polite religious greeting of praise but a political slogan meaning "Save us now." They wanted only what they were looking for, their deliverer. And as He went up that hill, out of the Kidron Valley, to the gates of Jerusalem, still they screamed, "Save us now." They put palm branches before Him just as they had done more than a hundred years earlier for Simon Maccabaeus and his son Judas, when they led the revolt against the Syrians. Everyone knew that here came the deliverer, the one man who could set them free from the current occupying forces—the Romans.

As Jesus came to the wooden gate, they just knew He would turn right and go toward the fortress of Antonia and deliver them from the Romans. No one dreamed for one moment that He would go to the left, into the temple, overthrow the tables of the money changers and set them free from themselves—rather than from the occupying forces. No one dreamed that Jesus wanted to bring a permanent revolution, not a temporary one; that He wanted to change life for all who would surrender to Him, not just for His chosen people; and that He was prepared to pay the ultimate price of death in order to bring freedom and a whole new life.

No one could have imagined that Jesus would sacrifice all His popularity and prestige just to fulfill His Father's purpose.

That's the stigma of being Christ. It's also the stigma of being a Christian. Most of us think that, as Christians, we're entitled to an easy life: a popular, free-wheeling existence leading to the joys of eternity and unending, unrestricted pleasure singing the praises of our undemanding God. How far from the truth can you get? No, following Jesus will mean taking up His cross and denying ourselves and following Him. There is a stigma. There must be a stigma. There always will be a stigma. You can't follow Jesus without being ready to live a life of sacrifice and surrender that comes from being a Christ-follower.

Very few people here in America are prepared to make that unwavering statement. We're all so fond of the notion that we must simply "accept" Jesus or "believe in Jesus," not even realizing that the devil does that; it certainly doesn't make him a Christian! Worse, we think we have to "receive Jesus," but He demands way more than that. Offering ourselves to Him, and taking up His cross, will be a journey of pain. And it takes a man who's walked with his Christ that way, who's lived that kind of life, to make those kinds of statements. R. T. Kendall has been my friend for more than a quarter of a century. He's a man for whom I would gladly lay down most things in order to serve and to honor, because he speaks the truth. In this book, again, R.T. says it as it is, lays it on the line, and demands that we learn what it means to follow Jesus.

And the stigma that we accept pales into insignificance when contrasted with the stigma that Jesus accepted for you and for me. That truth is life-changing; the message of this book could be life-changing, too.

But to have your life changed involves the risk of unpopularity—and now we're back where I started. Such is the call of God on the lives of those prepared to become true disciples of Jesus.

— *The Rev. Dr. Clive Calver*
Senior pastor, Walnut Hill Community Church

PREFACE

I suppose every author thinks that his or her latest book is their best and most important! I know that I almost always feel this way when I have just completed a book. People often ask me, "What is your best or favorite book?" To me, that is like asking, "Which of your children do you prefer?" I only know that I have seldom felt "fire in my bones" as I have in writing the book you now hold in your hands. I cannot adequately describe to you how deeply I feel about it. I just pray that you will feel something of this as you read on.

It was not easy to find people who would commend this book. This is because there is a stigma attached not only to the Gospel but also to the Holy Spirit. Some applauded what I say about the Gospel but wanted me to omit what I say about the Holy Spirit. Others were happy with my doctrine of the Holy Spirit but uneasy with the Gospel as I see it. I am therefore thrilled that there are some Christian leaders who are prepared to be identified with this book. I am singularly honored that Ken Costa, chairman of Alpha International and churchwarden of Holy Trinity Brompton—not to mention being one of England's most respected bankers—would write the foreword to this book.

This book is dedicated to Ricky and Sharon Skaggs—household names in America, especially to those who love the *Grand Ole Opry*. Ricky is a fellow Kentuckian, one of Nashville's greatest musicians and singers of bluegrass music. Most of all, Ricky and Sharon are stalwart believers who are absolutely unashamed of bearing the stigma of being Christians.

I pray this book will change your life.

— *R. T. Kendall*
Hendersonville, Tennessee
January 2011

INTRODUCTION

I am the way and the truth and the life. No one comes to the Father except through me.

— *John 14:6*

One of my friends said that about the most socially embarrassing thing you can be in contemporary Britain is a born-again Christian.

— *Quoted by James Runcie,*
son of the former Archbishop of Canterbury,
in The Scotsman, March 28, 2009

I write this book basically for one reason: that you will be *unashamed* to accept the scandal that arises from following Jesus Christ. More than that, you should become willing to embrace that scandal, to take it with both hands and rejoice in the privilege that you are a part of the greatest enterprise on the planet—namely, to be associated with the name Jesus Christ.

And yet there is a second word—*stigma*—that follows closely with the scandal inherent in the faith of Jesus Christ. We will look at both words. So whether it be the scandal that is associated with the Christian faith or that of being a Christian we are talking about something good and not bad. You should accept the scandal gladly. Why? As we will see in this book, its value is incalculable. It is one of the best things you have going for you. When you get to know God's *ways* and truly understand the Gospel, you will see that there would be something wrong if there were no scandal or stigma associated with the Christian message. The most predictable thing in the world is to be scandalized or stigmatized for your total commitment to Jesus Christ.

Both *scandal* and *stigma* are virtually pure Greek words. *Scandal* comes from *scandalon*. The meaning of scandal today denotes a sense of outrage or indignation. It is what offends the moral sensibilities of a society. The original usage referred to being caught in a trap or snare. It is usually translated "offense" or "stumbling block" in the New Testament. It is what puts people off; it can even cause you to stumble. The verb *scandalizo*—to offend—is used thirty times in the New Testament; the noun *scandalon*—offense—is used fifteen times. What is so offensive about the Christian faith can be briefly summed up: Jesus Christ is the only way to God and faith in the blood that He shed on the cross fits a person for heaven when they die. This teaching is an outrage to many and causes indignation that a person would truly believe this. And yet this message is what the Bible calls the Gospel. It is good news for sinners—but not righteous people.

The word *stigma* mainly means to suffer embarrassment for accepting the scandal of the Christian faith. This book is about feeling embarrassed, mostly for two reasons: (1) being a committed Christian in an age when it is not "cool" to be a Christian at all and (2) accepting the awkward consequences that often follow when you try to do God's will.

The word *stigma* is a Greek word that meant you were marked with a reproach. Paul said he bore in his body the "marks" (*stigmata*) of Jesus (Galatians 6:17). In ancient Greece it was like a tattoo, a distinguishing mark on your body—often used to identify a runaway slave. It was a mark of disgrace and shame. Paul borrowed the term to show he was unashamed to be a bond slave of Jesus Christ.

I have already prayed for you, dear reader, that as a consequence of reading this book you will be more willing than ever to accept the offense, the embarrassment or shame that comes with a commitment to Jesus Christ. Indeed, I pray that you will welcome it with all your mind, heart and strength and, like the early apostles, actually *rejoice* in the privilege of bearing that stigma for our Lord and Savior Jesus Christ.

Philip Yancey wrote the foreword to Jonathan Aitken's recent biography, *John Newton: From Disgrace to Amazing Grace*, in which Yancey pointed out that Newton did not try to defend himself but pointed to any good in himself as an outworking of God's grace.

> In doing so he stands squarely in the biblical traditions for its heroes include a murderer and adulterer (King David), a traitor (the Apostle Peter) and a persecutor of Christians (the Apostle Paul). Grace always has about it the scent of scandal.

1

PERSONAL BACKGROUND

Yet this is no cause for shame, because I know whom I have believed, and am convinced that he is able to guard what I have entrusted to him until that day.

— *2 Timothy 1:12*

Although my memory's fading, I remember two things very clearly: I am a great sinner and Christ is a great savior.

— *John Newton, 1725–1807*

My background prepared me for the day I would need to embrace the scandal of the Gospel for myself. I was born and raised in Ashland, Kentucky, located on the Ohio River in the eastern part of that state. In those days there were only forty-eight states. We had a slogan: "Thank God for Arkansas." This was because Kentucky was—at that time— 47th in educational standards. Arkansas kept us from being at the very bottom! But as far back as I can remember people from everywhere made fun of Kentuckians! Although I am now proud of being a Kentuckian, when I was growing up I sometimes felt a bit self-conscious when people categorized me by where I was from, especially when we went to Illinois on vacations. Being a Kentuckian became a part of my self-image, and this was not helped by my church background.

I was brought up in the Church of the Nazarene when Nazarenes were less sophisticated than they are today. Early Nazarenes were very expressive—shouting with excitement, even jumping up and down—when they felt God's presence. Their theology was more like the early Methodists. The ethos, preaching style and worship at my own church were influenced by the Cane Ridge Revival in central Kentucky. Ashland is just over a hundred miles from Cane Ridge, in Bourbon County, the historic spot where America's "second great awakening" took place in the early nineteenth century. This was the beginning of the phenomenon of "camp meetings." People came from five states in their covered wagons for fellowship and Bible study.

The Cane Ridge Revival reportedly began on a July Sunday morning in 1801 when a Methodist lay preacher stood on the top of a fallen tree before 15,000 people and preached a sermon from 2 Corinthians 5:10: "For we must all appear before the judgment seat of Christ; that every one may receive the things done in his body, according to that he hath done, whether it be good or bad" (KJV).

By the time he finished preaching several hundred people had fallen to the ground spontaneously and appeared to be unconscious for hours. Some panicked, fearing that these people had died (some reportedly only had a pulse rate of two beats per minute, which you cannot live on). But not to worry; hours later these same people came to, shouting at the tops of their voices, claiming full assurance of salvation and a heightened sense of the presence of God. The power of God swept through the camp, and hundreds of others fell. For four days there was not a time when there were not hundreds of people flat out on the ground. You could hear shouting, yelling, joyful screaming, also preaching and testifying, from a mile away. It was described as "the sound of Niagara." It is also probably one of the best explanations for the presence of a Bible Belt in America to this day.

In any case, that atmosphere swept all over Kentucky and its surrounding states and lasted for many years. I have no doubt that my church upbringing was influenced by Cane Ridge. In fact, I would say we were at the "tail end" of the momentum that had begun in the previous century. Nazarenes were called "Noisyrenes" by people in Ashland. You could hear them shouting if you walked near the church.

My first recollection of feeling embarrassed by my church was when—at about age twelve—one morning, on my way to school, a neighbor my age began taunting me in front of all the kids: "R. T.'s a Nazarene, R. T.'s a Nazarene." I was not laughing. It hurt. It was so embarrassing. From that day—which began an era that lasted for years—I was extremely aware of where I went to church and the way it was perceived by my friends.

I also had a strict upbringing. Perhaps too strict. I was not allowed to go to a cinema, to a circus or to the school dances. All my friends knew about it, and it was something I lived with throughout my childhood and teenage years. Others my age made fun of me. This self-consciousness was not improved when I was chosen by Dr. W. M. Tidwell, a visiting evangelist from Chattanooga, Tennessee, to be the chief illustration in his rendering of the parable of the wedding garment (Matthew 22:11–14), the basis for his sermon one Sunday morning. I was called into the pastor's office before the service, and Dr. Tidwell explained that he wanted me to illustrate the speechless person who had no wedding garment and who would be bound hand and foot and carried into outer darkness where there would be weeping and gnashing of teeth. Four men in the congregation were asked to carry me out at the appropriate moment in his sermon, which they did. They tied my hands and feet and carried me down the center aisle of the church and out the door. My fear was that someone outside the church would see me as they carried me out the door. The girl I fancied at the time lived across the street from the church and I could only think of how I would feel if she saw me carried out of the church by these four men. I had no idea what impact the sermon had on the congregation; I was only embarrassed.

But I later found out that the impact of the preacher's sermon was rather astounding. A holy hush fell on the crowd. Dr. Tidwell, aged eighty, announced, "Someone here is getting their last call." He warned the people to be sure they were saved and not to leave unconverted. He urged that person to come forward. It happened that my mother noticed that a young lady—Patsy (slightly older than I, but I knew her well)—had openly snickered and scoffed during the service, including when I was being carried out. My mother wondered at the time if Patsy was the very person Dr. Tidwell was referring to.

The next day, after I came in from my rounds delivering the *Ashland Daily Independent*, my mother said to me, "Have you heard about Patsy?" "No," I answered. "What are you talking about?" "Oh," said my mother, "as Patsy was walking home from school today, at 25th and Montgomery Avenue, a car ran into another car and it careened on the sidewalk. And Patsy was killed."

I was stunned, more shaken than I had ever been in my life. All the embarrassment I felt from the Sunday service was now gone. I never forgot it. Everybody who had been present remembered Dr. Tidwell's warning. All now knew it had to be Patsy. Her funeral was the most sobering funeral I ever attended. I could only think of how serious that Sunday morning service really was, and it taught me one thing: The stigma of being chosen to follow the Lord is an inestimable privilege. And though it hurts to be categorized and it can be totally embarrassing, it is a most wonderful honor to be called to bear any offense for Jesus Christ.

† PEER PRESSURE

A few years ago I returned to Ashland for a visit. I inquired about a number of people I used to know, including those who were the most popular during my school years and those who showed the greatest promise. I also asked about certain people who happened to be among those who had laughed at me. It was an enlightening moment. In many cases those who had either laughed at me or deserted me (because of my church) were the very ones who did not turn out very well. Concerning the most popular player on the football team, I was told, "He cannot even come to Ashland—the Mafia are looking for him." As for the star player of the basketball team, "He is divorced," they said, "living alone in a caravan on the edge of town, mainly sipping vodka all day, with nothing to live for." One person after another I asked about had not turned out well at all. And when I think of how important these people were to me then, it certainly gives a different perspective. The curse of peer pressure! The deceit of it.

And yet it is no different now. We want to be seen with the "right people," having a respectable job, owning a good home and maintaining a reputation of respect and honor. It is not cool to be a Christian, and being a committed Christian is costly indeed. But the cost is worth it; indeed, it is more precious than a million tons of the purest gold (1 Peter 1:7).

† THREE PRINCIPLES

If I could get the value of this theme over to you in this book, it comes to three things. First, it is a privilege to be scandalized or stigmatized for following Jesus Christ. We should welcome the stigma as we would look forward to the finest food, enjoy the loveliest scent or behold a most glorious sunrise. I guarantee that whatever stigma you bear for our Lord Jesus Christ, it will turn out to be the best thing that ever happened to you.

Second, I want this book to help you to see the utter folly of being concerned with a diminished reputation—if that comes about because of your obedience to the Lord Jesus. To let peer pressure—and what people think—motivate us or keep us from godly obedience is something we will live to regret. It is only a matter of time. As we see now how silly it was to let peer pressure affect us when we are young, so, too, when we are older. As I lived long enough to see the sad outcome of those who used to make fun of me, so you, too, will see that people who scorn you will be those who will eventually be ashamed—and found out. Third, the benefits that come from bearing the offense are incalculable. The good things when summarized come to two things: (1) a greater blessing from God here below and (2) a greater reward from God at the judgment seat of Christ—the very theme that Methodist lay preacher was emphasizing at Cane Ridge.

† WELCOME THE STIGMA

For this reason, I urge you again, learn to welcome the stigma with both hands. You will learn that the stigma first surfaces as a hidden blessing. You will develop an "instinct"—namely, an ability to discern that what seems so negative at first is in fact so promising. Yes, it hurts at first. But you will come to realize this is something you had better not let go of.

I like to compare the welcoming of the stigma to Jacob wrestling with the angel. The occasion was this: Jacob was minding his own business when, suddenly, someone pounced upon him—appearing as an enemy—and began to wrestle with him. Jacob did not realize it was an angel and the ordeal was certainly not something Jacob welcomed at first. But at some stage during the night he realized the person he was wrestling was not an enemy but a friend. He then saw the worth of this strange friend. He perceived in him a value so wonderful that Jacob made sure the opportunity did not slip out of his hands! The episode thus began with what seemed to be a very negative and most threatening occurrence, but once Jacob saw its worth he said to the angel, "I will not let you go unless you bless me" (Genesis 32:26). It was possibly the best thing that ever happened to him!

So, too, the stigma. The blessing behind being scandalized or bearing the stigma, then, is at first often concealed but—if welcomed and embraced—will develop into an incalculable blessing. There is no limit to the blessing that may come from this. For one thing, the very awareness that you are identifying with the mission of God on the earth is in itself immensely gratifying. But there is more. It could open many doors. It will lead to many opportunities. It will bring new friends. It will inevitably mean a greater anointing of the Holy Spirit, a blessing too rich to figure out. All this came because you embraced the stigma.

There is another relevant Greek word: *aischune*—"shame" or "disgrace." In the ancient Hellenistic literature this shame came from being found out by a judge; therefore, you were ashamed. Despite the promise that whoever believes on Christ shall not be "put to shame" (Romans 9:33), we are told to bear the cross—a mark of shame indeed. There was nothing more disgraceful than being sentenced to die on a cross. The one who was condemned to die on the cross had to carry it. And yet Jesus stated that we are to be unashamed of bearing the shame of His name. Think of that: being unashamed of the shame. Moreover, "If anyone is ashamed of me and my words," said Jesus, "the Son of Man will be ashamed of them when he comes in his Father's glory with the holy angels" (Mark 8:38). Later on, however, Peter and John actually *rejoiced* that they "had been counted worthy of suffering disgrace for the Name" (Acts 5:41).

† A FURTHER REMINDER OF THE PURPOSE OF THIS BOOK

My goal in writing this book is to bring you to rejoice as Peter and John did, when they embraced the privilege of suffering for the shame of Jesus' Name.

Speaking personally, I believe that God began preparing me—even at the most human level—to embrace the stigma from my earliest years. Even being a Kentuckian was part of it! This is why I mentioned my background—state and church—at the beginning of this chapter. What once embarrassed me I now embrace and treasure. I now regard the opportunity to bear the stigma, shame, disgrace or offense over whatever the Holy Spirit leads me to do as being more precious than words can describe.

I was the minister of Westminster Chapel for exactly 25 years (February 1, 1977, to February 1, 2002). My days at Westminster Chapel were not easy. Indeed, they were hard for me. I think that many a minister would, understandably, envisage being the pastor of Westminster Chapel as somewhat prestigious or glamorous. And that certainly was a part of the package. But that was not the whole story. One of the things I was required to do was to go out to the streets and start the Pilot Light ministry, and some felt it was outrageous for the minister of Westminster Chapel to be seen on the steps of the church giving out tracts to passers-by.

† THE BIRTH OF THE PILOT LIGHTS

Was I really *required* to do this? Yes. It happened one Friday night after forty or fifty of us headed toward Page Street in Westminster to invite people to church after getting them to answer our survey questions. It was the only way we knew to witness in those days. Arthur Blessitt, the man who has carried the cross around the world (he holds the Guinness book record for the world's longest walk), had excited all of us with the urgency of witnessing to the lost. Arthur and I were the last out and he followed me toward Page Street. On the way, he saw three young people standing next to the zebra crossing in front of the chapel. I thought, *Oh dear, Arthur is going to make us late getting to Page Street.* But two of these young people showed interest—and after several minutes they were praying to invite Jesus Christ into their hearts.

I said, "Arthur, we need to get to Page Street." But he saw another young man coming toward the chapel. I recognized this young man; he lived in Buckingham Palace Mews and used to come to the chapel. I felt Arthur was wasting his time. "We need to go this way, Arthur." Not listening to me, Arthur went straight up to this man. In a few minutes the young man was on his knees with Arthur, praying to receive Christ. After spending a little time with him, Arthur turned to me and said, "Dr. Kendall, I don't know where this Page Street is but you don't need to leave the steps of your church. You have the whole world passing here."

I was struck. It was the last thing I wanted to hear. But in those moments I had a vision—or something like that—of a pilot light, as in an oven or cooker: a light that never goes out. I conceived of the idea then and there of offering coffee on the porch of the chapel, witnessing to passers-by on Saturdays. I called a dozen or so people into the vestry and told them I was going to start a ministry in the streets. We would be Pilot Lights. On the first Saturday of June 1982 the Pilot Light ministry was born. Six people showed up and were ready to go. We never looked back.

On the night of our Farewell Service at Westminster Chapel, in January 2002, about two thousand people came to say good-bye to Louise and our family. Some eminent church leaders kindly spoke from the pulpit. But the high-water mark of the evening was when Charlie Stride, a Cockney taxi driver, gave his testimony. He told how he had found the Lord through the Pilot Light ministry on a cold Saturday morning several years before.

One Saturday morning I had the thrill of leading a Russian woman named Luba to Christ. She was a Jewish lady with almost no religious background. But she listened to the Gospel and prayed to receive Christ. I assumed that Luba, like so many we would pray with in those days, would never be heard of again. But she wrote me a letter. She had questions. I will never forget how she put it: "The people where I work now know I am a Christian and I do not want to do anything to let the Name down." By this I knew she was a truly converted woman. I was able to direct her to a church. She became a vital part of that church in Moscow. But the greatest part of this scenario is when she returned to London two years later as a translator with ten Russians. She had brought them to Westminster Chapel on a Saturday morning and said before them all: "Do for them what you did for me." She translated as I presented the Gospel. Several of them prayed to receive Christ. Luba still keeps in touch.

And yet you cannot imagine the stigma we all bore when we began the Pilot Light ministry. The neighbors who lived in Buckingham Gate resented our giving out tracts to them when they were out walking. Tourists on their way to see the changing of the guard at Buckingham Palace were annoyed when we mentioned Jesus to them. Most of all, some of the members of Westminster Chapel were indignant that we had started such a ministry. It seemed to offend everybody!

But it was one of the best things we did in our 25 years at Westminster Chapel. Hundreds and hundreds prayed to receive Christ over the next twenty years—from 1982 to 2002 (when I retired). Were all of them saved? Possibly not. But some of them were. One of them went into the Anglican ministry. On another occasion, an Anglican vicar in the north of England came to hear me preach in order to say to me, "I have wanted to meet you for years to tell you something; my daughter was brought back to the Lord through your Pilot Light ministry." I have run into countless people who have told of the blessing they received from it. The main consequence, however, next to praying with people to come to Christ, was this: the sweet presence of the Holy Spirit that came into the chapel over the ensuing years. Not only that, my anointing increased, fresh insights came, the unity of the membership returned and a healing presence came into the chapel.

The stigma was worth it. It will be worth it to you, too. After all, you cannot really avoid it—unless you decide you are not going to be a follower of Jesus. But if you are going to follow Him, get ready for it—the stigma, or scandal, is part of the package. What at first you may resent—and certainly underestimate—will be what you will eventually treasure and esteem more than you could have dreamed.

When it comes to giving, or tithing, you cannot out-give the Lord. He will bless you so much that it becomes almost selfish to give! When it comes to gratitude, or showing thanks, you cannot out-thank the Lord. As someone put it, "He can't stand praise," meaning that God just pours back more blessing upon you than ever. And when it comes to the shame of the Name, you cannot out-embrace the stigma of Christ. He will reward you so much that you will blush that you ever hesitated to accept the offense of the cross.

Perhaps you have let the Lord down at some point in your own past. You are so ashamed that you did this. You have wanted to do something that might redeem the past. Try this: Embrace the stigma of the Name. Let your past shame be eclipsed by embracing the shame of His Name—from this day forward. Take any opportunity to suffer for Jesus. It will come your way in a manner such that you know God's hand is on you, not only to give you a hope and a future but also to show how all things in your past—however shameful—will work together for good (Romans 8:28). That is what God does. He takes our sordid past and redeems it. This is partly done by letting us save face—by our embracing the cross. At last. Better late than never!

2

THE GOSPEL

I am not ashamed of the gospel, because it is the power of God that brings salvation to everyone who believes: first to the Jew, then to the Gentile.

— Romans 1:16

I hope for the day when everyone can speak of God without embarrassment.

— Paul Tillich, 1886–1965

Whatever happened to the Gospel?"

That question was the gist of my departing word at my farewell service at Westminster Chapel. I asked this because, it seems to me, the Church generally is interested in nearly everything else under the sun but the very reason God sent His Son into the world!

In Chapter 1 I also mentioned Charlie Stride, the taxi driver, who gave his testimony at our farewell service. One Saturday morning, a Pilot Light gave Charlie a tract I had written called "What Is Christianity?" Charlie reckoned he had received dozens of tracts over the thirty years he had been a taxi driver, but said this tract for some reason "shook me rigid." He came to the chapel the following Saturday morning, hoping someone would make him feel better and explain more about the tract, which he had read several times the previous week. They brought him to me. He was in tears. As Charlie and I sat in the backseat of his taxi, the first thing he said was, "If what you say is true in this tract, I am going to hell—is that right?" "I'm afraid so," I replied. I assured him that this destiny could be changed at once. I then presented the Gospel to him. It was the best news he had ever heard. Charlie was like a ripe fruit waiting to be plucked. He prayed to receive Christ that Saturday morning and became a trophy of grace.

I can never forget that a Christian printer did not want to print my little tract "What Is Christianity?" as I had written it because I said that Christianity is concerned mainly "about your death." He phoned to say I should write that Christianity is concerned "about your life." We went to a different printer.

To say that Christianity is concerned about your life would be absolutely true, by the way. Of course! No argument. But changing the words from "death" to "life" was nonetheless a subtle—even if unconscious—effort to destigmatize the Gospel, as if Christianity might be easier received this way. To mention "death" was considered too stark, or even needlessly offensive. The chances are, however, had I changed my words "concerned about your death" to "concerned about your life," Charlie Stride would not have been the slightest bit bothered with that pamphlet. Many tracts these days say little or nothing about dying or hell.

† PAUL'S EPISTLE TO THE ROMANS

The book of Romans is Paul's clearest, longest and most comprehensive statement on the Gospel. Whereas other epistles largely answered questions his converts had asked, Paul had not been to Rome. So in his letter to the Romans, he articulated the Gospel in a breadth and depth not seen in his other letters. He apparently wanted Christians in Rome to know what he believed before he arrived there and so he wrote as he did—leaving nothing out. As soon as Paul wrote that he was "not ashamed of the gospel" (Romans 1:16), he began to unfold it: "For in the gospel the righteousness [Gr. *dikaiosune*—which also means justice] of God is revealed" (Romans 1:17). Then he added, "The *wrath of God* is being revealed from heaven . . ." (Romans 1:18, emphasis mine). Few people seem to talk about how closely connected God's wrath and justice is to the Gospel—right at the beginning of this epistle. The Gospel was literally launched in Romans in the immediate context of God's righteousness, justice and wrath.

I do not mean to be unfair, but I suspect that the Gospel is preached many, many times throughout the world without its being even remotely connected to God's justice or wrath. John Newton's second verse from "Amazing Grace"—"'Twas grace that taught my heart to fear"—would seem odd, foreign or out of place to many Christians today. This is largely because they never feared much in the first place. Some might say that it is not really the Gospel that is taught if it is not attached to God's justice. I could readily make a case for saying that. It is certainly not the "purest Gospel," Martin Luther's phrase in introducing Romans. But God is gracious and saves people through *any* part of His Word, not always requiring that you and I are totally "sound" when we present the good news of Jesus Christ. I can never forget my own theological background before I came to grasp God's grace; I am not sure any of my old pastors were as sound as Paul was.

Martin Luther referred to John 3:16 as the Bible in a nutshell: "For God so loved the world that he gave his one and only Son, that whoever believes in him shall not perish but have eternal life." The words "shall not perish" is a direct reference to your destiny after death. The assumption is that all are perishing; believing the Gospel is the only thing that can save them and keep them from perishing. Furthermore, the words "Just as people are destined to die once, and after that to face judgment" (Hebrews 9:27) point to the heart of the matter: We are all going to die and we all must face God at the judgment seat of Christ.

What we do with the message of the Gospel determines whether we spend eternity in heaven or hell. By the way, does this offend you? If so, you can see why we are talking about this word *stigma*.

Before we can embrace the scandal of Christianity we should know: (1) what we are embracing; (2) why there is such a scandal;

and (3) what is at the heart of it. The heart of the scandal is the Gospel of Jesus Christ. In a word: that God sent His Son into the world to die on a cross in order that we might go to heaven and "not perish" in hell. The word *gospel* means "good news" (Gr. *euaggelion*—"good tidings," "good news"). The good news is that Jesus died and that His death turned God's wrath away from our sins and satisfied His justice. You would have thought that such good news would surely be welcomed by all! But, sadly, not all receive it gladly.

My old friend Henry Mahan used to say that "when the pure Gospel is preached as it is to men as they are it will save some and condemn others but it will accomplish God's purpose."

The Gospel is often perceived as *bad news* before it becomes good news. That is the way it was with Charlie Stride. The thought of going to hell is bad news. The thought of standing before God without being clothed in the righteousness of Jesus Christ is bad news. Martin Luther believed that we must know God as an enemy before we can know Him as a friend.

Why does the stigma come into the picture because we mention the Gospel? It is because the true Gospel as unveiled in the New Testament—unembellished and undiluted—initially offends. For those who do not receive it, it *continues* to offend. The Gospel is by nature *offensive*. It offends people for more than one reason but especially to say that Jesus Christ is the only way to God (John 14:6) and that Jesus is the only way to heaven (Acts 4:12). Some are annoyed at the thought that the Gospel relates more to life after death than what happens to our lives in the here and now. To embrace the Gospel as unveiled in the Bible is therefore to anticipate the offense that comes with it. I wish it were not that way. But it is.

When Paul Tillich longed for the day that everyone could speak of God without embarrassment, he envisaged a God who does not offend. This is why he came up with a novel definition of God and a new definition of faith. Tillich called God "the ground of all being." This means that the same God who is the ground of all living things in the universe (e.g., plants, animals) is the same One who is the ground of all religions—whether Christian or not. His view is known as panentheism ("all in God"). There would be no stigma whatever in a "God" like that, for this would imply a God who is at the basis of every religion—Christian, Hindu, Islam or any cult. Tillich defined faith as "ultimate concern." With this definition everyone has faith. He admitted that even an atheist could have faith by this definition. So if everybody accepted Tillich's definition of God and faith it is quite likely that everyone could speak of God without embarrassment! There is no stigma in a God who is equally the ground of all religions.

The scandal associated with the true Gospel, however, is three-fold. First, it is attached to the belief that all people need to be saved in the first place. Second, that the one and only true God sent His one and only Son to die on a cross for our sins. Third, that reliance upon Jesus Christ and His death on the cross is the only way to God and to heaven. The purpose of this chapter is to explain the Gospel. It will become clearer why it is offensive.

When Paul said, "I am not ashamed of the gospel," we should probably note that he did not say, "I am not ashamed of the *prosperity* gospel," for I doubt there would be much offense in this. Appealing to people's wish for financial gain is certainly a convenient entry point. But that is not the Gospel. Then Paul added, "because it is the power of God for the *salvation* of everyone who believes" (emphasis mine). Some indeed might wish he had said the Gospel "is the power of God to bring you financial blessing—or physical healing." But he did not say that. When Paul envisaged going to Corinth, he "resolved to know nothing while I was with you except Jesus Christ and him crucified"

(1 Corinthians 2:2). Had he said, "I resolved to preach a gospel of health, wealth, prosperity and healing," I can safely guarantee that there would have been no offense. People would line up for days in order to be healed or be prosperous. Who can blame them? But that is not the essential message of the Gospel.

† WHATEVER HAPPENED TO THE GOSPEL?

Read the books that come off the press. Read the Christian books. The Christian magazines. Watch religious television. Listen to the sermons. Look at the sermon titles. Far too many today write about or preach almost everything but the Gospel. How often do you hear the Gospel? Near our home in Hendersonville, Tennessee, were these words on a church's billboard: GOD IS CRAZY ABOUT YOU.

A year or so ago I disappointed a number of my friends when they wanted me to get on a bandwagon and endorse a particular minister who was preaching every night in Lakeland, Florida. He was taking the country by storm. I also received a letter from an English friend: "I hear revival has broken out in Lakeland." The meetings in Lakeland during part of 2008 were on TV every night—*live*—so when I was home I watched it night after night. I felt uneasy the more I watched it. But some of my friends were endorsing this ministry and were urging me to endorse it, too. I began to get phone calls and emails that I should back this man. I tried hard to listen and enjoy him but I could not. Why was I unable to approve of this man and his ministry? Mainly for this reason: Never in my lifetime have I seen such an opportunity to present the Gospel to the whole world. Imagine this! Here was an unprecedented opportunity to preach the Gospel to many nations of the world simultaneously. What is more, millions were watching and enthralled. Why? The testimonies of healing, miracles and reports of people being raised from the dead! Of course, there was no way to prove the healings or these alleged resurrections. But my friends assured me they were all true. If they were true, was this not good enough reason to endorse this man's ministry? No. Why not? Because never once when I listened did he preach the Gospel! I listened night after night, waiting for one thing—to hear the Gospel mentioned, that God sent Jesus Christ into the world to die on a cross for our sins. Had he said this even once I would have had to climb down from my stand. But he never did. What is more, I wondered if the person preaching even knows the Gospel. There was no hint that he *understood* the Gospel in the first place. For if he had, it was bound to leak out one way or another, sooner or later. There is one thing certain about someone who knows the Gospel; it has a way of coming out! You can't *not* mention it if you believe the Gospel that Paul had in mind. I knew, sadly—and tried to get my friends to see—that this man did not preach the Gospel. But I went further; in the magazine *Ministry Today* I even said the Lakeland phenomenon was "not of God," which shocked quite a few people. But King Saul's efforts to kill young David were certainly not of God, and yet Saul prophesied during the same time (1 Samuel 19:19–24). How could this be? Because the gifts and calling of God are "irrevocable" (Romans 11:29); even if someone is not following God rightly, their spiritual gifts still function. The person whose spiritual gift functions is not necessarily the person God approves.

Sometime later it came out that the Lakeland preacher had a very questionable lifestyle, and soon afterward he divorced his wife to marry his secretary, with whom he was having an affair. By then, some people decided that perhaps I had got it right after all. Which did not bless me. "Why did it take a man's immorality to convince you?" I asked. "You should have known that this whole thing was not of God even if he was not living in immorality."

These meetings had even been heralded by some "prophets" as the "last day ministries" we have all been waiting for, the final and ultimate "end time revival" to precede the Second Coming. Wrong. I knew that if God were behind these meetings the first thing the Lord would do would be to raise up a person who preached the Gospel of His one and only Son. There is no way God could be the architect of these meetings and the Gospel be totally absent! The meetings were all about signs and wonders, miracles, healings and unusual "words of knowledge" (when sicknesses and conditions were revealed to the evangelist). Some were indeed stunning. They seemed real. And perhaps some of them were. It is even possible that some of the people were healed; God might honor the people's sincerity and their faith. That would not be surprising.

But if God were going to command the attention of the whole world you can be sure He will put at the top of the list of priorities *the reason He sent His Son into the world to die on a cross for our sins that we might go to heaven and not to hell.* That is the reason Jesus came and died.

Mind you, I believe in healing. We had surprising healings in Westminster Chapel. I could write a book on healing, and may do so one day.

† DESTIGMATIZING THE GOSPEL

But the Gospel of Christ is not primarily about physical healing and hardly about prosperity. Inject prosperity into the Gospel and the offense largely disappears. Appealing to people's fleshly natures to get them to become Christians is an attempt, consciously or unconsciously, to destigmatize the Gospel. Everybody wants to be prosperous. I said to a waitress during the time I began writing this book, "We are getting ready to ask God's blessing on our food; how can we pray for you?" She replied, "Money." I then prayed that God would bless her financially. But the point is, if you promise people money if they will come to Jesus, there will be no offense.

There is no offense in a gospel of healing, although I repeat that I believe in healing. People will line up by the thousands and wait indefinitely to be prayed for in order to be healed. I do not blame them. I have certain things I would like prayer for. I would walk a hundred miles if I knew I would be healed totally of certain things that give me concern.

But the Gospel of God is about *salvation*. That is why Paul added, "It is the power of God for the *salvation* of everyone who believes" (emphasis mine). And sadly people by and large are not interested in this. But they will be. It is appointed to all of us that we will die—and after that, the judgment. All are unanimous on this: We are all going to die. But the main thing is, what happens then? Answer: the judgment (Hebrews 9:27). It is only a matter of time before the Gospel—and the Gospel alone—will be the most important thing in the whole world to you.

Some readers may know that I had a friendship with the late Yasser Arafat. On my first of five visits with him at his headquarters in Ramallah, I said, "*Rais* [Arabic for president], the most important question anybody can ask you is not whether you get Jerusalem or the Israelis get Jerusalem, but where will *you* be one hundred years from now?"

3

THE MOST IMPORTANT QUESTION

If you declare with your mouth, "Jesus is Lord," and believe in your heart that God raised him from the dead, you will be saved.

— *Romans 10:9*

For we are to God the pleasing aroma of Christ among those who are being saved and those who are perishing. To one we are an aroma that brings death; to the other, an aroma that brings life. And who is equal to such a task?

— *2 Corinthians 2:15–16*

The most important question for Yasser Arafat, any head of state or you is: Where will *you* be one hundred years from now? Will you be in heaven, with God, or in hell? This question may offend you. If so, it proves my point regarding the offense of the Gospel. People by nature want to think of the "here and now" rather than eternity. I understand this. In any case, the kindest question anybody can put to you is this: *Do you know for certain that, if you were to die today, you would go to heaven?* Do you? Would you?

And if you were to stand before God (and you will), and He were to ask you (and He might), why He should let you into His heaven, what would your answer be? What would you say? Do bear with me. What exactly *would* you say to God if He asked you why He should let you into His heaven? Suppose it were for *real* and you knew that if you did not come up with the right answer you would have to go somewhere else, somewhere you do not want to go? So what would you say?

There will be readers who do not need this chapter. The irony is, they will perhaps enjoy it most of all! Truly saved people never tire of hearing the Gospel. I recall early days at Westminster Chapel when one of the deacons—M. J. Micklewright, aged eighty—would come into the vestry after a Sunday evening service exclaiming, "Well, I got saved all over again tonight!" What he meant was not that he was just converted or that he had been backslidden; he meant that hearing the Gospel brought him right back to when he first accepted Christ. It was reliving the experience. This happens to millions.

† HOW TO KNOW YOU ARE SAVED

Let me tell you how I know I will go to heaven when I die. It is because it is *free*. Yes! Whereas the wages of sin is "death," the "gift of God is eternal life in Christ Jesus our Lord" (Romans 6:23). Eternal life is a gift. Not earned. Not merited by anything we can do. God *gives* it to you.

You may be surprised that heaven would be a free gift. But that is the only way it could be. This is because if it were offered to us on the basis of our personal merit, the standard is so high nobody would ever be allowed entrance! God requires sinless perfection for entrance into heaven. His eyes "are too pure to look on evil," God "cannot tolerate wrongdoing" (Habakkuk 1:13). God requires perfection of mind, tongue and body 60 seconds a minute, 60 minutes an hour, 24 hours a day, 365 days a year. Are you perfect? Would you qualify to enter heaven if the requirement were your own sinlessness?

The issue becomes more relevant when you realize what the Bible says about sin. "All have sinned and fall short of the glory of God" (Romans 3:23). "There is no one who does not sin" (1 Kings 8:46). "If we claim we have not sinned, we make him out to be a liar and his word is not in us" (1 John 1:10).

To summarize: In order to qualify for heaven you must admit that you are a sinner. This does not mean you are an Adolf Hitler or Saddam Hussein. We all sin. Our thoughts are so often sinful. Lust is a sin. Telling a lie is a sin. Not forgiving another person is a sin. The truth is, we all sin.

The problem becomes even more acute when you realize what the Bible says about *God*. The Bible basically says two things about God: that He is merciful and that He is just. By merciful this means He does not want to punish you. By just this means He must punish you. *Do you have any idea how God could be both just and merciful at the same time?* There is only one answer: He punished His Son for our sins in order that He might be merciful to us. The Lord laid on Him the iniquity of us all (Isaiah 53:6). His justice has been satisfied so He can be merciful to you. That is the heart of the Gospel.

This then is why God sent Jesus Christ into the world. You need to know who Jesus was—and is. Jesus was—and is—God. "In the beginning was the Word, and the Word was with God, and the Word was God" (John 1:1). The "Word" describes Jesus in eternity before He entered the Virgin Mary's womb and took on a body (Luke 1:34–35). Jesus was—and is—equally man. "The Word became flesh and made his dwelling among us" (John 1:14). Jesus therefore was—and is—the God-man. He lived without ever sinning—in thought, word or deed—60 seconds a minute, 60 minutes an hour, 24 hours a day, 365 days a year for the whole of His life. Indeed, although He was tempted just like we are He did not ever sin (Hebrews 4:15). "He committed no sin" (1 Peter 2:22). This could not be truly said of any other human being. But it is what made Him a sacrifice without any blemish; hence He was called the "Lamb of God, who takes away the sin of the world!" (John 1:29).

His sinless life was lived for us and for His Father. He was our substitute the whole of His life. He was taking our place from the moment of His birth to the moment of His death. All He did was for us and for His Father—fulfilling the Law for us and satisfying God's justice (Matthew 5:17). Jesus even fulfilled righteousness by being baptized for us (Matthew 3:15), and in the end He died for us (Romans 5:8). When He uttered the words, "It is finished" (John 19:30), the Greek is *tetelestai*—a colloquial expression in the ancient marketplace that meant "paid in full." That is what happened when Jesus died: He paid the debt we owe to God. In full. There is nothing left for us to pay.

† Two Things

Jesus' sinless life and sacrificial death did essentially two things for us—here are two words for your theological vocabulary: (1) *expiation,* meaning atonement (making amends)—what the blood of Christ does for *us,* washing away our sins; and (2) *propitiation*—meaning that His blood turned away God's wrath from us and satisfied His justice. The first shows what the blood does for us; the second shows what the blood of Jesus does for *God,* turning His wrath away from our sins.

On the third day after He died Jesus was raised from the dead. Jesus is the only person to have been raised from the dead who is eternally alive. His resurrection, moreover, is proof that each of us will be raised the *same person*—not another person or animal in a future life (as some teach). Furthermore, we are destined to die "once" (Hebrews 9:27), which also shows that you will not have another death in a future life. *This life is it*—the only life you will ever have. Never forget: Jesus actually *died.* Islamic teaching says that Jesus did not actually die on the cross. Yasser Arafat said to me, "We believe that Jesus ascended to heaven." I replied, "Yes, but He *died* first, rose from the dead and *then* ascended to heaven." Whether Jew, Gentile, Hindu, Baptist, Methodist, Mormon, Buddhist or Muslim, we must affirm that Jesus died and rose from the dead in order to be saved (Romans 10:9).

As long as you are relying on your good works to get you to heaven, you are still as lost as ever. I'm sorry, but I do you no favor not to tell you that. Even if you are basically a good person, have been baptized, joined a church, were brought up in a Christian home, have given millions to charity or have done your very best to impress God, if you are relying on those things and not on faith in Jesus, you are not saved. I'm sorry, but that is the way it is.

If our works could have saved us, God would not have sent His Son into the world to die on a cross. He sent Jesus because He is the only person who could save us and His death was the only way to satisfy God's justice. But once you have accepted two facts—(1) that you cannot save yourself by good works and (2) that only Jesus Christ can save you—you are ready to move to the next stage: to accept the gift. A gift may be accepted or rejected. It is not yours until you accept it. I used to say to people on the streets of Westminster, "You may go to Victoria station and believe that train on platform 8 is going to Brighton, but it will not take *you* to Brighton unless you get on the train." So, too, with the gift of God which is eternal life: You must accept the gift.

† TOO GOOD TO BE TRUE?

If you say, "This is too good to be true," I reply, "Good for you in saying that." For until this Gospel seems too good to be true, you probably have not heard it! It probably shows "the penny hasn't dropped." You probably do not really get it until you realize this seems too good to be true. This is why we call it the Gospel—*good news*. It is not good news if I am told that I have to save myself by my good works. It is not good news if I am to believe the only way to God is through effort, merit and being good enough. How do you ever know you have reached the standard of being good enough? So if you say, "This is too good to be true," it shows the very reason Paul asked the question, "Shall we go on sinning so that grace may increase?" Why did Paul raise that question? Because it seemed to some that a person continuing in sin—as long as he or she accepted the Gospel—was acceptable. Wrong. This is called antinomianism (against law)—the idea that it does not matter how you live after you are saved. Dr. Martyn Lloyd-Jones used to say, however, that if the Gospel we preach is not vulnerable to the *charge* of antinomianism it is probably because the true Gospel was not preached! This is what I meant by saying that until the Gospel seems too good to be true, you probably have not heard the Gospel yet. But, as Dr. Lloyd-Jones equally said, if you think that the Gospel allows you to continue to sin deliberately, you *still* have not understood it. I will return to this important point below.

It is not good news, then, if I am told I must be "fit," "prepared" or that I have had to "turn from every known sin" *before* I am qualified to trust Jesus' death. If turning from every known sin is a prerequisite to being saved, I ask first, how can I ever be sure I have in fact turned from every known sin? Second, will I not invariably be trusting my having turned from sin rather than relying on the blood of Jesus? My eyes will forever be upon myself, my faithfulness and obedience. I will also feel I must keep myself saved by maintaining a particular righteous standard. There will be no true assurance, only frustration, in trying to please God by being good enough.

† WHAT OFFENDS ABOUT THE GOSPEL?

Mind you, there are admittedly those who find it offensive that we are saved entirely by what Jesus has done for us. You would think they would be thrilled. And yet I admit that many people have not been taught anything else. Indeed, the most natural feeling in the world is to feel we must earn our way by being good. Christianity is the only religion in the world that promises we get to heaven as a result of what God does for us, not what we do for God. Therefore people who hope to get to heaven by their good works say they feel unaffirmed or not sufficiently dignified by such an easy way to heaven. They feel better if they have to do something, pay a price or be sufficiently qualified to be saved. It gives them a feeling of worthiness. They do not like to "get something for nothing," so they feel better if they have had a hand in the whole process. I'm sorry, but that is sheer self-righteousness. It is sinful pride that makes us want to get to heaven by good works.

Therefore, for some the stigma in relying completely and totally on Jesus' death lies not in embarrassment about what being a Christian might entail, but in the *easiness* with which the Gospel allows a person to be saved.

In my old church in Ashland there was great stress on people giving up smoking, drinking, going to cinemas or even (for women) wearing makeup, in order to be saved. The person therefore felt "saved" if they quit smoking or stopped wearing lipstick. And if they started smoking again, you assumed they were no longer saved. That was the consensus in my old church in those days. You could tell a backslidden woman when she began to wear makeup again. She was no longer a Christian, we thought. I am sorry for all those to whom this seems ridiculous, but that kind of thinking was a part of my own theological background. This is why I can smell a "works"-oriented Gospel a mile away. The thought of trusting Jesus' death on the cross sadly did not come into the picture—unless you made a clean break with anything worldly *first*. The problem was (obviously) that *good works* determined whether you had a *warrant* to be saved. How anybody can call that kind of thinking "good news" is beyond me. Even if they disavow the extreme kind of legalism I have just described, the same is true: If you have to be rid of all that is wrong before you have a warrant to rely on Christ's death, this makes *works* the ground of your assurance and salvation. For Paul said, "It is by grace you have been saved, through faith—and this is not from yourselves, it is the gift of God—*not by works, so that no one can boast*" (Ephesians 2:8–9, emphasis mine).

The word *grace* means unmerited favor. The difference between grace and mercy is: Grace is getting favor you do not deserve; mercy is not getting the justice you do deserve.

Many of the old hymns reflect what I am teaching here. I thank God for them. For example:

> Just as I am, without one plea
> But that Thy blood was shed for me,
> And that Thou bidd'st me come to Thee,
> O Lamb of God, I come.
>
> Just as I am, Thou wilt receive,
> Wilt welcome, pardon, cleanse, relieve;
> Because Thy promise I believe,
> O Lamb of God, I come.
>
> — *Charlotte Elliott, 1789–1871*

> Let not conscience make you linger,
> Nor of fitness fondly dream;
> All the fitness He requireth,
> Is to feel your need of Him:
> This He gives you;
> 'Tis the Spirit's rising beam!
>
> — *Joseph Hart, 1712–68*

> Enough for me that Jesus saves,
> This ends my fear and doubt;
> A sinful soul I come to Him,
> He'll never cast me out.
> I need no other argument,
> I need no other plea;
> It is enough that Jesus died,
> And that He died for me.
>
> — *Lidie H. Edmunds, 1851–1920*

These hymns suggest "good news," very good news indeed. It seems too good to be true that you and I, miserable and unworthy sinners, can come directly to Christ in faith and trust what He did—His living and dying for us—and be saved forever. That, dear reader, is why it is called *good news.*

You will ask—you certainly should—why live a holy life then? I answer: It is like a P.S. at the end of a letter, saying, "Thank You, Lord, for saving my soul." You spend your life thanking Him. Sanctification—the process by which we are made holy—is essentially a *life of gratitude.* We are not saved because we are sanctified; we live a holy life *because* we have been saved. Holiness of life is gratitude and is not helping you get to heaven.

And yet the scandal of the Gospel is that God will take the most wicked sinners and save them in a second—if they rely entirely on Jesus Christ. Indeed, a person can be saved in the final moments of life—and go to heaven. And it is also true: You can live a good moral life for the whole of life—and go to hell. Yes, that is offensive. This is why the Pharisees were given no hope of being saved as long as all they did was for people to see (Matthew 23:5), whereas the worst sinners were promised salvation if they repented (Matthew 9:13).

✝ REPENTANCE

Repentance (Gr. *metanoia*—"change of mind") means making a U-turn in your thinking, saying "I was wrong," "I am sorry." It is climbing down from having denied that Jesus is God, and saying, "Yes, Jesus is God." It is climbing down from being so self-righteous, then saying, "I am a sinner. I am sorry for my sins." Making that kind of confession means you are ready to accept the gift. Not because you are good enough but because you know you are certainly not good enough! That is the preparation you need—to know your utter unworthiness and to feel your need of Him. Are you ready? Would you like to accept this gift? If so, pray this prayer if you mean this with all your heart:

Lord Jesus Christ, I need You. I want You. I know I am a sinner. I am sorry for my sins. I know I cannot save myself. Wash my sins away by Your blood. I now rely on Jesus. I welcome Your Holy Spirit into my heart. As best as I know how, I give You my life. Amen.

If you have grasped what I have said above and prayed this prayer from your heart, you are a saved man or woman. You are as saved as I am. You will go to heaven when you die. What you have done is to embrace God's one and only way to be saved. You have also, even if you did not realize it, embraced the stigma of Jesus Christ. I will therefore ask you to tell at least one other person that you prayed this prayer. Your relationship with other people has now changed. Begin reading your Bible every day. If you do not have one, get one! Pray daily. You get to know the Lord more intimately when you spend time with Him. Find a church where the Bible is preached and Jesus Christ is honored. There will be some who will congratulate you. Thank God for this.

But most people out there will not be impressed with what you have done. Expect this. Do not be surprised when they think you have lost your head or have been unwise. You have been very wise indeed. The beginning of wisdom is the fear of the Lord (Proverbs 1:7).

Perhaps many who have read this chapter did not need to pray the prayer I offered above. You will therefore know why I inserted it in this part of the book.

† WHAT WE CAN EXPECT MANY PEOPLE TO SAY TO US

When we make the claim that Jesus Christ is the only way to be saved, we will often get the retort, "So you think you are the only one who is right." We must be careful here. Our reply is this: We are only taking Jesus' words seriously. He is the One who made the claim, "I am the way and the truth and the life. No one comes to the Father except through me" (John 14:6). It is not so much that I got it right but that I believe Jesus got it right—and I am siding with Him! As followers of Jesus we embrace Him as a person—but also what He said. We would not be true followers of Jesus if we did not accept what He taught. So our reply to the critics is this: It is not that I think I am right but that Jesus is right. We also affirm what the earliest Church confessed, "Salvation is found in no one else, for there is no other name under heaven given to mankind by which we must be saved" (Acts 4:12).

The thing we must avoid is destigmatizing the Gospel, that is taking the stigma out and still calling it the Gospel. This I fear is what the Church at the present time, speaking generally, has done. With the destigmatizing process has come a loss of the Church's power. I call on every reader of these lines to be bold and uphold the pure, unembellished Gospel of Jesus Christ— precisely as it is taught in the New Testament. "Jesus Christ is the same yesterday and today and forever" (Hebrews 13:8). This means being unashamed of the Gospel. Jesus said, "If anyone is ashamed of me and my words in this adulterous and sinful generation, the Son of Man will be ashamed of them when he comes in his Father's glory with the holy angels" (Mark 8:38).

4

THE OFFENSE IN THE OLD TESTAMENT

As she kept on praying to the LORD, *Eli observed her mouth . . . [and] thought she was drunk and said to her, "How long are you going to stay drunk? Put away your wine."*

— *1 Samuel 1:12–14*

"I will become even more undignified than this, and I will be humiliated in my own eyes. But by these slave girls you spoke of, I will be held in honor."

— *2 Samuel 6:22*

Bearing the stigma because of obedience to God, whether through embarrassment or extreme suffering, is nothing new. The ways people suffered in ancient times varied from person to person and from generation to generation. The people of faith described in Hebrews 11 knew great suffering for relying on the Lord and obeying His word. Some miraculously avoided death by faith; others accepted death by faith and were tortured (Hebrews 11:33–35). When we say "Yes, Lord," we sign a blank check and let Him fill in the amount! Perhaps the one thing all those described in Hebrews 11 had in common was that not a single one of them had the luxury of repeating the calling or mission of a previous person of faith. They were all "pioneers," accepting the challenges—and stigma—that God had for them, stigmata nobody before them had faced.

† ABEL

The ancient stigma begins with Abel—the first martyr for Christ and also the first "prophet" (Luke 11:50–51). His offense was offering the firstborn of his flock, which God approved. He was persecuted by his brother Cain who had offered fruits of the soil. God was not happy with Cain's offering, although Cain was given a second chance. Cain rejected the offer and murdered Abel (Genesis 4:3–8).

The stigma remains the same to this day. It is the offense of the Gospel, namely, that God is not looking to our works or what our hands produce but only to the sacrifice of the cross where the Lamb of God suffered. Like it or not, God is only satisfied by a blood sacrifice—that of His one and only Son.

> Nothing in my hand I bring,
> Simply to Thy cross I cling;
> Naked, come to Thee for dress;
> Helpless, look to Thee for grace;
> Foul, I to the fountain fly;
> Wash me Saviour, or I die.
>
> — *Augustus Toplady, 1740–78*

This way of salvation is offensive to the world and embarrassing to the Christian. But we accept the stigma with both hands.

† NOAH

One of the funniest comedy routines I ever watched was Bill Cosby mimicking Noah. Cosby imagined a neighbor approaching Noah, asking what was going on there in Noah's front yard. "I'm building an ark," said Noah. The sketch lasted several minutes and Cosby demonstrated how ridiculous Noah must have appeared, saying, "It's going to rain." Hilarious though this was to watch, I do not think Noah found his own plight very amusing! Imagine the embarrassment of building this huge monstrosity of a ship that would float on water, hundreds of miles inland, at a time when it had not even rained!

Noah followed Enoch in Hebrews 11. Enoch "walked with God" (Genesis 5:24); Noah "walked with God" (Genesis 6:9). But Noah was not translated like Enoch was but was ordered to build an ark and save his household. There was no precedent for this. What a stigma Noah bore before all the people. But he moved with fear to save his family and, in doing so, became "heir of the righteousness that is in keeping with faith" (Hebrews 11:7).

† ABRAHAM

God told Abraham to leave his country, and Abraham did so (Genesis 12:4), but he "did not know where he was going" (Hebrews 11:8). What an embarrassment this must have been for him. What evidence or sign could he point to in order to make his decision look good?

That was only the beginning. Abraham had been promised that his seed would become a great nation. But Abraham had no heir as he grew older. One day God said "count the stars . . . so shall your offspring be." Had Abraham been like some of us he would have said to God, "You must be joking." This is the reaction some have to the Gospel; they cannot believe that we will go to heaven by faith alone! But Abraham "believed the Lord," was credited with righteousness because of his faith alone, and became Paul's model for the teaching of justification by faith (Genesis 15:2–6; Romans 4:3). As the Gospel leads to more stigmas, so, too, with Abraham's continued challenges.

† LEAH AND RACHEL

It is impossible to say which of Jacob's two wives suffered more—Leah or Rachel. Jacob loved only beautiful Rachel but was tricked by Laban into marrying Leah, who was plain. Leah's stigma was that she was unloved by her husband Jacob, but bore him children. Rachel's stigma was that she was barren. "Give me children, or I'll die!" said Rachel to Jacob, who replied by saying that God was the one to blame (Genesis 30:1–2).

Sometimes God allows a stigma—an embarrassment you cannot explain away—to offset things in our lives that might divert us from putting God absolutely first. We all tend to need something negative in our lives, that is, something from God that gets our full attention to make Him our utmost priority.

Which was harder to accept—being beautiful and loved but barren, or being plain and unloved but able to have children? Leah kept hoping with each child that her husband, Jacob, would finally love her. He never did. Leah became reconciled to this and said with her last child, "This time I will praise the LORD" and named him Judah (Genesis 29:35). Rachel finally bore Jacob two sons—Joseph and Benjamin—but died when Benjamin was born. The irony is, the unloved Leah—so unappreciated by Jacob—bore two sons who did more for Israel and the Church than the other sons combined: Levi and Judah. Levi became the tribe of the priesthood; Jesus was born into the tribe of Judah.

† JOSEPH

Joseph was falsely accused by Potiphar's wife. She wanted Joseph to go to bed with her. He refused. "Hell [has no] fury like a woman scorned," said William Congreve. She told her husband that Joseph had tried to rape her. Joseph was thrown into a dungeon (Genesis 39:7–20). How about that as a stigma—being a Hebrew in Egypt and put in prison there for a crime you did not commit? Peter said,

> It is commendable if someone bears up under the pain of unjust suffering because they are conscious of God. . . . If you suffer for doing good and you endure it, this is commendable before God. To this you were called.
>
> — *1 Peter 2:19–21*

Not in spite of this but because of it, Joseph was eventually made prime minister of Egypt, almost literally overnight, because he alone in Egypt could interpret Pharaoh's dreams. Pharaoh said,

Can we find anyone like this man, one in whom is the
spirit of God? . . . There is no one so discerning and wise
as you. . . . All my people are to submit to your orders.
Only with respect to the throne will I be greater than you.

— *Genesis 41:38–40*

This was no doubt very gratifying to Joseph. But the chances
are that he would have far preferred to have his name cleared
regarding the charge of being a rapist. That never happened, as
far as we know. Sometimes we bear a certain stigma throughout
our lives and have to wait until we get to heaven to have our
names cleared.

† MOSES

Moses bore the stigma of choosing "to be mistreated along with
the people of God rather than to enjoy the fleeting pleasures
of sin." This was regarded as "the reproach of Christ" (ESV),
regarding "disgrace for the sake of Christ." You could call Moses
a pragmatist. He regarded this stigma as having "greater value
than the treasures of Egypt, because he was looking ahead to
his reward" (Hebrews 11:25–26).

After Moses was accepted by his fellow Israelites he endured
one stigma after another—all because his leadership was misunderstood. Things did not move fast enough for the people of
Israel, which was hard for Moses. God even made a proposi-
tion to Moses—He would destroy the Israelites and start all
over again with a new people. "No!" said Moses, "what will
they think about your great Name in Egypt?" Moses interceded
for those who were unappreciative of his leadership (Numbers
14:13–19), which shows the greatness of Moses.

The value of the stigma is incalculable. Moses made a shrewd,
pragmatic decision when he left Pharaoh's palace. But he became

a type of Christ when he interceded for an ungrateful people. This showed him to be the greatest leader of people ever, but also indicated that he was possibly the noblest person who ever lived until Jesus was born. It began when he embraced the stigma.

† HANNAH

The mother of Samuel was barren for a long time. Somewhat like the rivalry between Leah and Rachel, Hannah had to cope with her husband's other wife. Like Rachel, Hannah was loved and preferred by her husband. This love, however, did not compensate for her pain, which was caused by her inability to have children. Her husband felt he should mean more to her than "ten sons." He did not understand her pain—or embarrassment. The truth is, "The LORD had closed Hannah's womb" (1 Samuel 1:3–8). It is a reminder that God could be behind a stigma like this and it therefore means a sovereign strategy is behind what is happening—and that there is a wonderful plan in the making.

Hannah went to the temple to pray. "In bitterness of soul" she wept and cried out to God. As she prayed, the priest Eli observed that her lips were moving but her voice was not heard. He thought she was drunk—which was a further, though temporary, stigma for Hannah to endure. "Put away your wine," Eli said to her (1 Samuel 1:14). It reminds us of the disciples on the Day of Pentecost, when the Jews accused them of being drunk. Hannah was able to convince Eli that she was very sober indeed and that she longed for a son. She vowed that if God gave her a son she would give him to the Lord—a promise she absolutely kept after Samuel was born and weaned.

When God strategically closes a womb, it is because He has a great purpose in view. Hannah's stigma and intercession led to the great prophet Samuel.

† SAMUEL

Samuel arrived on the scene in an era when "the word of the LORD was rare" (1 Samuel 3:1). It shows God's love for Israel and how He had raised up Hannah in order to give Israel its greatest prophet since Moses. The greatest thing that can be said of a prophet is that "none of his words fall to the ground" (1 Samuel 3:19). But the greater the stigma, the greater the anointing; so, too, the greater the anointing, the greater the suffering.

The people wanted a king "as all the other nations have" (1 Samuel 8:5). This displeased Samuel. He warned them that this was wrong and they would live to regret it. It was an embarrassment that they paid no heed to his wisdom. But Samuel's genius was listening to God so that he did not take their rejection personally. When God told him to give them a king, Samuel went all out to find them the best man around—Saul, of the tribe of Benjamin. Sadly, King Saul became yesterday's man in a very short period of time. Samuel never went to Israel to say, "I told you so," but sought the next person God had in mind—now that the kingship was going to be a permanent establishment. Samuel found David (1 Samuel 16).

† DAVID

When David finally succeeded in bringing the Ark of the Covenant to Jerusalem, he was so excited that he shamelessly threw aside his kingly robe and danced before the Ark wearing a linen ephod. You could almost say he lost his head—but he knew full well what he was doing! The Ark—the symbol of the presence of God—meant more to David than anything. This revealed his heart of hearts. You could also say he invited a stigma—which he bore gladly. It deeply offended his wife Michal, the daughter of King Saul. When David returned home, she was waiting for him and said, "How the king of Israel has distinguished himself today, going around half-naked in full view of the slave girls of his servants as any vulgar fellow would!" (2 Samuel 6:20).

I will never forget preaching on this passage at Westminster Chapel. I called the sermon "Finding Your Friends." David knew who his real friends were—those who rejoiced in the return of the Ark as he did! He said to his wife that he had done all this "before the Lord" and that he would become "even more undignified than this, and I will be humiliated in my own eyes. But by these slave girls you spoke of, I will be held in honor" (2 Samuel 6:21–22). I would regard this as David's finest hour.

† MORDECAI

The unsung hero of the book of Esther was Mordecai, Esther's relative, who adopted her and brought her up to respect God's ways. Sometime after Esther was made queen, Mordecai did something that was very strange. When King Xerxes honored Haman the Agagite, for some reason Mordecai refused to honor Haman. He was the only person who would not obey the king's command and kneel down to pay Haman honor. It made no sense at the time. He accepted a stigma—an embarrassment to himself but also to Esther, who could not understand what was going on. We can only conclude—because we know how things eventually turned out—that Mordecai was led by God and saw what nobody else could see: that making Haman angry would finally lead to Israel's glory. It was an extremely risky thing to do.

I am amazed how, day after day, Mordecai intentionally infuriated Haman. When Haman found out that Mordecai was a Jew, it gave Haman the excuse he needed to get even with Mordecai. He manipulated Xerxes to put his seal on an edict that would destroy all Jews. This led Mordecai to go into fasting and wearing sackcloth at the king's gate. Word of this got to Esther, who was very distraught. Mordecai then told her of the Jews' fate—if God did not intervene. After all, Esther was also a Jew and she, too, would be killed. He said those never-to-be-forgotten words: "And who knows but that you have come to your royal position for such a time as this?" She promised to approach the king, doing something very precarious since she risked losing everything if the king had not sent for her. But she promised to do it and said, "And if I perish, I perish" (Esther 4:14–16).

The result was that Mordecai was vindicated, Haman was hung on the gallows he himself had prepared for Mordecai and Esther and all the Jews were spared. It began with the courageous acceptance of a stigma nobody could figure out. But after all, a stigma is an embarrassment you cannot explain away.

† THE PROPHETS

When Jesus said that being insulted because of Him catapulted people into the category of the prophets, adding that their reward in heaven would be "great" (Matthew 5:11–12), we may conclude we are to understand an unusual anointing and a lot of suffering. He also spoke of a "prophet's reward" (Matthew 10:41). This suggests a wonderful reward indeed. But it implies extraordinary suffering. Persecution. Being misunderstood. Remaining unvindicated for a good while. We referred above to Hebrews 11, which lists those who by faith escaped the sword but also those who "were tortured," "faced jeers and flogging" or "chains and imprisonment," or were "put to death by stoning" or "sawed in two" (vv. 33–37).

Isaiah is a favorite prophet of many. But how many of us are aware of his stigma? For a time Isaiah was made to take off the sackcloth from his body and the sandals from his feet. He went around "naked and barefoot." Then the LORD said,

> As my servant Isaiah has walked naked and barefoot for three years as a sign and a portent against Egypt and Cush, so shall the king of Assyria lead away the Egyptian captives and the Cushite exiles, both the young and the old, naked and barefoot, with buttocks uncovered, the nakedness of Egypt.
>
> — *Isaiah 20:3–4, ESV*

According to a long-standing legend in Israel, Isaiah was the one described in Hebrews 11:37 as "sawed in two."

Jeremiah endured various kinds of stigmas. Apart from the physical suffering he endured (e.g., Jeremiah 37 and 38), the charge of treason was laid at his feet. That is the kind of stigma no Israelite would welcome. But Jeremiah prophesied what was thought unthinkable by everyone—Jerusalem not only could but would be taken by the Babylonians. "Never!" said the Jews. There was unanimity among the Jews that God would always— forever and ever—protect Jerusalem: It was special, the apple of God's eye. But Jeremiah stuck to his guns: "It will be given into the hands of the king of Babylon" (Jeremiah 32:36). It happened just as he said (Jeremiah 52).

Ezekiel was told to lie on his left side and bear the sins of Israel for 390 days, then lie down again, "this time on your right side, and bear the sin of the house of Judah. I have assigned you 40 days." Not only that, but "I will tie you up with ropes so that you cannot turn from one side to the other until you have finished the days of your siege" (Ezekiel 4:4–8). I know a lot of people who would like to have a prophetic gift like these men. But do we accept the stigma and suffering that will almost certainly accompany such a gift?

Daniel the prophet had three friends—Shadrach, Meshach and Abednego. They are the ones who "quenched the fury of the flames" when they refused to bow down to the golden image of King Nebuchadnezzar (Daniel 3:16–25; Hebrews 11:34). As for Daniel, he also stigmatized himself by going against the unjust decree not to pray to his God. After the decree was issued, Daniel "went home to his upstairs room where the windows opened toward Jerusalem. Three times a day he got down on his knees and prayed, giving thanks to his God, just as he had done before" (Daniel 6:10). He was thrown into the lions' den but was miraculously delivered, having "shut the mouths of lions" (Hebrews 11:33).

What a stigma it must have been for Hosea to accept the command, "Go, marry a promiscuous woman and have children with her, for like an adulterous wife this land is guilty of unfaithfulness to the LORD" (Hosea 1:2). Later, God said to him, "Go, show your love to your wife again, though she is loved by another man and is an adulteress. Love her as the LORD loves the Israelites, though they turn to other gods" (Hosea 3:1). One of God's inexplicable ways is to require things of us that make no sense at the time.

When we accept the stigma that comes with the territory of obedience to God, we do not know how things will turn out. As we have seen, some escaped death "by faith" while others "by faith" went to their torturous death. As I said, we sign a blank check to God and let Him fill in the rest.

The writer who wrote Hebrews 11 did so to show that faith was not a New Testament innovation but was the common denominator of all obedient followers of God. Every single one of them did what they did by faith. As for those people, "the world was not worthy of them" (v. 38). They are a part of that "great cloud of witnesses" who, just maybe, can see what is going on here below. We are inspired to "throw off everything that hinders and the sin that so easily entangles" in order to run the race "marked out for us" (Hebrews 12:1).

When we sign that blank check, we do not know what is marked out for us. But I want to be in that race. I would love to be a successor of those described in Hebrews 11—whatever it takes or whatever the cost. I only have one life. Only what is done for Christ will last. As C. T. Studd (d. 1931) put it: "If Jesus Christ be God and died for me, then no sacrifice is too great for me to make for him."

Will you sign that blank check?

5

EMBRACING THE SHAME OF THE NAME

And they departed from the presence of the council, rejoicing that they were counted worthy to suffer shame for his name.

— *Acts 5:41, KJV*

The people where I work [in Moscow] now know I am a Christian and I do not want to do anything to let the Name down.

— *Luba, new Russian convert*

May I remind you that I write this book so that you will be unashamed to accept the stigma of following the Lord Jesus Christ. But this chapter perhaps goes beyond that—I hope that you will actually *welcome* the stigma. It is one thing to endure it, another to welcome it. Why welcome it? This pleases the Lord. It shows you are counting it "pure joy" when you face bearing the stigma (James 1:2). But welcoming the stigma also demonstrates that you regard this as a privilege. The sooner everyone can see this, the better.

It is such an honor to be chosen to bear the stigma of the Lord Jesus. Yes, chosen. We are saved in the first place because we have been chosen. "You did not choose me, but I chose you and appointed you so that you might go and bear fruit," said Jesus (John 15:16). "We love because he first loved us" (1 John 4:19). This is why we are called God's elect, or "chosen" (Romans 8:33). No one is saved by accident. Those who believe, said Luke, had already been "appointed for eternal life" (Acts 13:48).

Among the chosen, however, are some who perhaps have been doubly chosen—if I may put it that way—that is, they are not only saved but were also chosen to suffer. It is a double privilege. Perhaps all Christians are chosen to suffer. After all, said Paul, "it has been granted to you on behalf of Christ not only to believe in him, but also to suffer for him" (Philippians 1:29). But not all suffer to the same degree.

I only know that if I am persecuted for my faith it is because I am *called* to suffer. Like conversion, it is no accident. Although I could say the devil is behind persecution, I see it as something

God has allowed. It is not unlike Paul's "thorn in the flesh." Although this thorn was a "messenger of Satan," Paul saw God as being at the bottom of it all (2 Corinthians 12:7–10). Therefore, whether it be a thorn in the flesh or persecution from the world, it means you and I have been selected for a very high honor. When we suffer because of our obedience, it is because God has special plans for us. It is part of our inheritance, which God chooses for us (Psalm 47:4). If persecution comes to you and me, then, we should therefore take it with both hands. If we suffer in this way it means it is His idea, so I urge you to welcome such suffering with all your heart.

† THE ANOINTING

At stake in this discussion is your anointing. This is a word that can be used in more than one way. It basically refers to the power of the Holy Spirit *on* or *in* us. Jesus said in the synagogue in Nazareth, "The Spirit of the Lord is *on* me, because he has anointed me to proclaim good news to the poor" (Luke 4:18, emphasis mine). John said, "You have an anointing from the Holy One," that it "remains *in* you, and you do not need anyone to teach you" (1 John 2:20, 27, emphasis mine). John meant that the anointing in us immediately recognizes *truth* and detects error. We wish for a greater anointing in order to be better equipped for God's service—not only to distinguish truth from error but to be more empowered to exercise our gifting.

The anointing is what enables your gift to function with *ease*. When I struggle in what I am trying to do, it is probable that I have moved outside my anointing. God will never promote you or me to the level of our incompetence. When I am operating within my anointing, I am at ease, not fatigued but thinking clearly and at peace. When I go outside my anointing, I lose peace, cannot think clearly and get easily irritated and tired. And yet the greater the anointing in us the greater our ability to sense that anointing—so we will operate within it and not outside of it. Best of all, we want more of the Spirit of God in order to excel in what we do with ease. In short, I want a greater anointing of the Holy Spirit. Don't you?

There is one "catch": the likelihood of *suffering*. I wish it were not so! But suffering has a way of emerging when our anointing increases. And yet suffering is also a hint that a greater anointing may be on the way. So if it is a greater anointing I want, I am going to welcome suffering.

I repeat: The greater the suffering, the greater the anointing; the greater the anointing, the greater the suffering. By this I simply mean that the promise of a greater anointing is *on offer* when you suffer for the shame of Jesus' Name. But it is also true that if you have been given a great anointing, you will almost certainly find that, sooner or later, suffering goes with it. Therefore, do not expect a great anointing without the suffering because suffering— almost always—does seem to be connected with greater anoint- ing. It was because of God's unusual calling with regard to Paul— "visions and revelations from the Lord"—that he was given that aforementioned thorn in the flesh (2 Corinthians 12:1, 7).

Why must suffering be a part of the "anointing package"? First, it is because suffering may promise further anointing if we do not disdain that suffering. In other words, if you want your anointing to increase, suffering helps to maintain the level of anointing you presently have but also promises an ever-increasing anointing. But only if you dignify the suffering. You dignify suffering by regarding the trial as pure joy, as in James 1:2. Suf- fering is a test from God to see how much you really do desire a greater anointing of the Spirit.

Second, suffering is a part of the anointing package because it is so humbling. Paul admitted that his own thorn in the flesh was to keep him from being conceited (2 Corinthians 12:7). This is partly the reason why anointing and suffering go together. The greatest saints you read about and hear about are just as human, vulnerable and fragile as you and me; their successes could easily go to their heads if they were not humbled along the way to keep them from taking themselves too seriously.

It is an indisputable fact that the greatest saints in ancient times and in Church history endured great suffering. Do not pray for a greater anointing if you are unwilling to have greater suffering. And if you should be among those who want the kind of faith described in Hebrews 11, expect the kind of suffering that accompanied these people as well. But when a greater anointing is your true inmost desire, you should find yourself welcoming any measure of suffering because such suffering is God's hint that an even greater anointing is on the way.

There are few verses in the Bible that have gripped me like Acts 5:41. Charles Spurgeon once said that when a verse gets a hold of you, the chances are you have got hold of it. If he is right, here is a verse I have truly got hold of. I cannot be sure why this verse grips me as it does. I have not even remotely suffered as Peter and the apostles did. At best I have had a mere taste—perhaps a teaspoonful—of what they experienced. But there are occasions, for some reason, when I cannot read Acts 5:41 without coming to tears.

Imagine that someone actually rejoices when suffering *shame*! The word "disgrace" or "shame" in Acts 5:41 comes from the Greek *atimasthenai*, which means "being dishonored." Picture this: A person is dishonored by the most reputable and authoritative legislative body in the land—and rejoices in the shame of it! If someone were shamed or dishonored today by Parliament or Congress, could he or she *rejoice*? In the case of Peter and the apostles it was the powerful and prestigious Sanhedrin that dishonored them. And yet they were thrilled. I suspect they had to pinch themselves that they were so "lucky"—if I can be forgiven for using that word! Not because they were dishonored but because that dishonor came over *the shame of Jesus' Name*.

Why did the apostles rejoice? Let us try to get to the bottom of the reason these men rejoiced when they were so shamed. This is surely unusual, if not unnatural. The most natural reaction in the world to being shamed is feeling negative and embarrassed, if not also feeling sorry for yourself. Whatever would cause someone to *rejoice* in disgrace?

Here is what happened. The occasion of the disciples rejoicing in being shamed for Jesus' Name began with a miracle. Peter and John were instruments in the extraordinary healing of a forty-year-old handicapped man who had never walked. As soon as Peter said, "In the name of Jesus Christ of Nazareth, walk," instantly the crippled man started walking and jumping (Acts 3:8). No one questioned the authenticity of this miracle. "Everyone living in Jerusalem knows they have performed a notable sign, and we cannot deny it," the unbelieving Jews admitted (Acts 4:16). Whereas this miracle ought to have made the authorities vindicate the early Church and accept their credibility—if not also affirm Jesus as Messiah—they dug in their heels and officially warned the apostles not to speak or teach in Jesus' name. But Peter and John replied, "We cannot help speaking about what we have seen and heard" (Acts 4:20).

After this warning, the Church turned to God in prayer. When they finished praying, the very place where they were meeting was "shaken" and they were given a fresh infilling of the Holy Spirit (Acts 4:31). The Church was endued with more power, resulting in one couple being struck dead for lying to the Holy Spirit (Acts 5:1–10), the apostles were held in high esteem by the ordinary people (Acts 5:13) and people were healed right, left and center as well as being delivered from evil spirits (Acts 5:15–16). The authorities were filled with jealousy and put the apostles in the public jail (Acts 5:17–18). But they were miraculously let out of jail by an angel of the Lord—and continued preaching (Acts 5:19–20). The apostles were then made to appear before the Sanhedrin. Peter took advantage of the occasion to preach the Gospel (Acts 5:29–32). They would have been put to death had not Gamaliel, an honored teacher of the Law, intervened with a persuasive speech. The apostles were then flogged and ordered "not to speak in the name of Jesus," and were let go. This brings us to Acts 5:41: "The apostles left the Sanhedrin, rejoicing because they had been counted worthy of suffering disgrace for the Name."

Why then were they rejoicing? There were several ingredients that lay behind their joy—all coalescing simultaneously. First, they had been freshly filled with the Holy Spirit and had a renewed empowering not unlike what they initially experienced on the Day of Pentecost. The filling of the Spirit always results in supernatural joy. This joy had brought about the charge that the disciples were drunk on the Day of Pentecost. I doubt that hearing the disciples speak in a foreign tongue and yet understanding it in their own language caused people to scoff (Acts 2:4–6). That aspect of the phenomena of Pentecost would have been sobering to observers. It was the high level of joy in those who had been filled with the Spirit that led mockers to say, "They have had too much wine" (Acts 2:13). There is nothing like the joy of the Holy Spirit to enable a person to rejoice in adversity. That is the first explanation for their rejoicing when being demeaned: a fresh filling of the Holy Spirit.

Second, the apostles now had a momentum of powerful exploits that prepared them for the ordeal of the Sanhedrin's wrath. As we saw above, the filling of the Spirit resulted in supernatural happenings all around Jerusalem—the miraculous healings, plus their being let out of jail by the angel. They fearlessly proclaimed to Sadducees and Pharisees, "We must obey

God rather than human beings!" then preached the Gospel with power and ease (Acts 5:29–32). It was obvious that they were entirely at home in speaking as they did. What would have been daunting, if not unthinkable, without the anointing—speaking to high-ranking Jews as they did and facing the threat of the Sanhedrin—was now carried out with utter ease. It reminds me of the boldness of three Hebrews—Shadrach, Meshach and Abednego—facing Nebuchadnezzar's fiery furnace: "We are not careful to answer thee in this matter" (Daniel 3:16, KJV). The irony is, these three Hebrews faced an enemy outside the ancient covenant; the disciples faced fellow Jews who should not have been enemies—but now were.

Third, the apostles were rejoicing because they knew without doubt that God was totally with them and on their side—and not with the Sanhedrin. That alone was enough to catapult them into sheer bliss. Not to mention the confidence it gave them. Were they feeling pain? Of course. The flogging wasn't fun and the official order from the Sanhedrin—not to speak in the name of Jesus (Acts 5:40)—was unpleasant to hear. But the disgrace did not bother them. The shame rolled off like water from a duck's back.

For when we know without doubt that God is with us, there is a level of joy and assurance promised to us that goes beyond the natural level. "If God is for us, who can be against us?" exclaimed Paul (Romans 8:31). There is nothing that parallels the excitement of knowing that God is with us, behind us, backing us and is the sole architect of what is going on around us. Normally the apostles—being Galileans, uneducated and unsophisticated (Acts 4:13)—would have been intimidated by the Sanhedrin. But not this time. They were rejoicing. They were experiencing the approval that comes from God alone, the very thing the Pharisees sadly did not even consider (John 5:44). The approval of God more than compensated for the physical pain of the flogging and the disapproval of the Sanhedrin. Whereas the Pharisees and Sadducees were probably saying among themselves, "That will show them—we'll teach them a thing or two," the truth was that all the apostles were thrilled to their fingertips that they were given the privilege to suffer shame for Jesus' Name.

Fourth, they knew, too, that Jesus taught, "Blessed are you when people insult you, persecute you and falsely say all kinds of evil against you *because of me*" (Matthew 5:11, emphasis mine). As we will see further below, there can be suffering that we unnecessarily bring on ourselves—and is hardly because of Jesus' Name. We have all done that. I know I have. But not the apostles—at least this time! They *knew* that what was now happening was insults and persecution *because of Jesus*. After all, God did the miracle that started all this, not them. The Gospel was not their idea; it was born in heaven. So when they were commanded to stand before the Sanhedrin they were standing on their rightful authority in their words to the Sanhedrin and bubbling over with joy on their faces.

They therefore qualified for this promise: "Great is your reward in heaven, for in the same way they persecuted the prophets who were before you" (Matthew 5:12). Their reward may not be on earth but was great in heaven—whether that means in heaven's eyes at the moment or the promise of a great reward when they get to heaven. This would also mean even greater anointing than ever for them here below, even if that particular thought did not enter their minds at the time. They certainly knew they had obeyed the Lord, and that thought was sweet indeed. There is nothing to compare to knowing you have done the right thing. Peter would later write, "If you are insulted because of the name of Christ, you are blessed, for the Spirit of glory and of God rests on you" (1 Peter 4:14).

The word "blessed"—in Peter's use here and in the Beatitudes (Matthew 5:3–12)—comes from the Greek *makarios*, which means "happy." But it may also be translated "congratulations." That is the shout of the angels to us—*congratulations,* if we could hear it—when we are bearing the stigma for our Lord Jesus Christ. Yes, congratulations. For great is our reward in heaven. The stigma promises dividends that cannot be calculated here below.

Fifth, partaking of the sufferings of Christ—which they were experiencing—made the person of Jesus very real to them, apart from the promise of a greater anointing. Perhaps I ought to have listed this first. The "Spirit of glory and of God rests on you," says Peter (1 Peter 4:14). The very participating in Christ's suffering is an inestimable privilege, even if there were no greater anointing or blessing down the road for us. This is why Paul could say that he wanted to know Christ and the power of His resurrection "and"—*and*—"participation in his sufferings" (Philippians 3:10). There is a certain fellowship with the risen and ascended Lord that comes from partaking in His sufferings. It is an inner joy and sense of God—when He is so *real*—that you would not trade anything in the world for it. The disciples were experiencing this as they departed from the council. The presence and sense of God was so real to them. In a word, experiencing the sufferings of Christ as they did made Jesus extremely real to them.

But there is a sixth reason they were rejoicing. In all this they realized God had given them a *second chance.* For all I know, this could have been the main thing on their minds. The realization to them may have seemed too good to be true. They all knew that they had blown it the first time. Especially Peter. Peter sincerely believed that he loved the Lord more than the other disciples did. He wanted to outdo them in devotion. When Peter said to Jesus, "You shall never wash my feet," he thought he was being more respectful. Then when Jesus said, "Unless I wash you, you have no part with me," Peter responded, "Not just my feet but my hands and my head as well!" (John 13:8–9). Right after that,

Jesus said to Peter, "Before the rooster crows, you will disown me three times!" (John 13:38). Peter honestly thought Jesus had got it wrong. But a few hours later Peter denied knowing Jesus. When the rooster crowed, Peter remembered Jesus' words and "wept bitterly" (Matthew 26:75). But it was not only Peter who let the Lord down. When Jesus was arrested, "*all* the disciples deserted him and fled" (Matthew 26:56, emphasis mine).

They all felt so horrible after forsaking Jesus and denying Him as they did. They must have wanted another opportunity to show their love for the Lord. But would they get it? Yes. This is partly what lay behind their rejoicing that they were "counted worthy" of suffering for the shame of His Name. They who proved themselves so unworthy were now counted worthy. Second chance. Wow. What a wonderful thing this was for them!

Question: Have you wished for a second chance? Have you let the Lord down? Do you feel awful for the way you have behaved since you have known the Lord? Would you give anything to prove your love for Him by having a second chance? The God of the Bible is the God who gives second chances. The "word of the LORD came to Jonah a second time" (Jonah 3:1). The same Jonah who refused to "go" but said "no" began praying for a chance to do the very thing he had previously refused to do. When God came to him a second time, "Go to the great city of Nineveh," they were the sweetest words Jonah ever heard! "Jonah obeyed the word of the LORD and went to Nineveh" (Jonah 3:3).

If you have been a Jonah—or a Simon Peter—God will give you a second chance. First, be sure that you have truly repented of what you did that displeased the Lord. Second, just wait. The time will come when you will be given an opportunity to prove your repentance. God did this for Peter and the apostles. He will do it for you.

Do not be ashamed of the Name. Embrace it—and the stigma that comes with that Name.

6

NAME-CALLING

The disciples were called Christians first at Antioch.

— *Acts 11:26*

If you suffer as a Christian, do not be ashamed, but praise God that you bear that name.

— *1 Peter 4:16*

We seldom get called what we prefer to be called by those who object to the way we choose to follow Jesus Christ. Many names that began as a term of insult or derision eventually gain respectability—and lose the stigma originally attached to them. The name *Christian* was not meant to be flattering to the followers of Jesus when they were first called that, but in time it gained respectability. But as long as it was offensive they were urged not to be ashamed of it.

A later example was in the name *Puritan*. Those in the Church of England in the sixteenth century who felt that the Reformation had not gone far enough in England were called "Puritans." This name was applied to certain preachers and their followers because they wanted to purify the church from certain traditions that seemed wrong to them—such as lighting candles, upholding certain ceremonies and the wearing of vestments. They emphasized personal regeneration, sanctification as the ground of assurance of salvation, strict morality, personal and household prayers and especially preaching from the Bible. But those who were nicknamed Puritan, like William Perkins, rejected this appellation as a "vile term" and resented being called that. But the derisive term stuck and eventually was used to describe those who became heroes to this movement. It eventually became a badge of honor.

John Wesley, his brother Charles and George Whitefield formed the "holy club" at Oxford. During the time John Wesley taught at Lincoln College he met for set times of prayer with Whitefield and Charles. Because of the methods they used they were called "methodists." Those who were called that did not like it. It was not meant to be a compliment. But when revival broke out years later through the preaching of Whitefield and John Wesley—combined with the hymns of Charles—their followers continued to be called methodists and the movement became the Methodist Church. By the time it went to America the name was owned and used by its members and had become respectable.

Baptists had come along early in the seventeenth century to emphasize baptism *after* coming to personal faith, thus rejecting infant baptism, although they first baptized by sprinkling. Baptism by immersion was brought over to England from Holland in the seventeenth century. Because of the emphasis on baptism following their profession of faith, many who had been baptized as infants were baptized as adults when they believed for themselves. They were called "anabaptists"—a derisive label—which meant rebaptizers. The Baptists countered that they did not rebaptize, that if you were baptized as an infant it should not properly be referred to as baptism in the first place. Baptism, they argued, was only *true* baptism when it followed your acknowledgment of a personal faith. Baptists in England were still called Anabaptists for years—possibly to identify them but also to keep them stigmatized and in their place. The term *Anabaptist*, however, eventually fell by the wayside. The movement managed to shed a derisive term and became known as Baptists. What began as a stigma, including baptism by immersion, was destigmatized by time.

Being called something they did not appreciate was also true of the Quakers. This word was applied not as a compliment but to describe a practice among certain people who followed the teachings of George Fox. It is said that through Fox's preaching people began to quake—tremble. In the course of time people were expected to tremble before the word of God. I have long suspected that there was something quite genuine about the original quaking—that there was a sense of God in Fox's preaching that caused the trembling unexpectedly and without working it up. The problem was that in many cases it became a required occurrence, whether or not it was precipitated by the presence of God. One of the best-known proponents was William Penn, who several years later established the colony of Pennsylvania. Quakers today, however, prefer to call themselves the Society of Friends. A different movement sprang up in the next century, called Shakers, who were called that partly for the same reasons as the Quakers. All that is left of this movement is a little town called Shakertown, Kentucky.

So then with the name *Christian*. It was what disciples of Jesus were eventually called, and first at Antioch (Acts 11:26). Until then they were apparently known as followers of the Way (Acts 9:2), a description that continued for a while (Acts 19:9, 23). There was another term—*Nazarene*. Paul was called a "ringleader of the Nazarene sect" (Acts 24:5). That term did not stick and possibly did not truly surface again until my old denomination was founded in Pilot Point, Texas, in 1907. But the term *Christian* stuck. However, it was at first a term of derision. We know this because Peter wrote that if you "suffer as a Christian"—which meant if you are called that because you follow Jesus Christ— "do not be ashamed, but praise God that you *bear that name*" (emphasis mine). It therefore became a badge of highest honor.

The name *Christian*, however, at some point ceased to be a term of derision and became a label proudly worn by followers of Jesus Christ. Not only that, it became the standard appellation for whether you are a true follower of Christ and are indeed regenerate. Many now take the term *Christian* for granted and even apply theological standards to people in order to judge whether or not they are *truly* "Christians"—i.e., saved. The name *Christian* is used today to describe people who were born into Christian homes, whether or not they had personal faith in Jesus, those who have been baptized, those who join a church and those who identify with a certain culture (as Palestinian Christians) or even a political movement.

The Cane Ridge Revival, to which I referred earlier—called America's "second Great Awakening"—thrived partly under the preaching of Barton Stone. At its height, in the first three or four years of the nineteenth century, there was minimal emphasis on doctrine or church affiliation. Before the revival there were denominations who aggressively emphasized certain teachings—Baptists emphasizing baptism and the security of the believer, Presbyterians preaching predestination, Methodists stressing a certain view of sanctification. But historians have observed that at the peak of the revival—when there was a high level of the Holy Spirit's power—those distinctions simply did not matter! Barton Stone said what mattered is only whether you are a Christian. Yes! It sounded so good. But before the first decade was over Stone founded the "Christian Church"! Surprise, surprise, it became another denomination.

Why do we engage in name-calling? It may be a subconscious attempt to elevate ourselves and make our opponents appear inferior. We do it when we disapprove of people, are disgusted with them or lose our tempers. In the Sermon on the Mount Jesus warned against using derogatory substitutes for a person's own name. Calling a person "Raca" (an Aramaic term of contempt) was the equivalent of saying "you moron, you idiot" or calling a person "you fool!" which was used in ancient times to judge a person's character or motive (Matthew 5:22). Our Lord will not allow us to treat people like that. If they treat us like that, we must turn the other cheek and accept it. But we are never to engage in name-calling.

Our name is our identity. God took names seriously. He wants us to take names seriously—and to do nothing to put a person down by negative name-calling or by hurting another's reputation. A good name is a wonderful possession, better than great riches (Proverbs 22:1). God Himself calls us by our name (Isaiah 43:1). Shakespeare said, "Who steals my purse steals trash. . . .'Twas mine, 'tis his, and has been slave to thousands; but he that filches from me my good name robs me of that which not enriches him and makes me poor indeed." In a word, let them call you whatever they choose—and accept it as part of the stigma—but never, ever do the same to them. We almost never get called what we would choose. I loved it when I was once introduced by an Anglican vicar near Manchester, England, as a "no-label man." Wow. I wish that one would stick! But I know better, and the way I am referred to by some people these days makes me cringe and is very embarrassing. But never mind, they will probably do it to you, too. God will level out things at the judgment seat of Christ and, frankly, that gives me more hope than you can possibly imagine!

Elisha the prophet was not amused when some boys jeered at him and said, "Get out of here, baldy!" He got immediate revenge when two bears mauled the boys (2 Kings 2:23–24). I only know that you and I are to bear the stigma without expecting God to step in at once to clear our names.

When I think of how black people in America have suffered—including so many black Christians—I am saddened and sobered. What is so appalling is the way white Christians, not only in the South, have called black Christians by the N word and felt nothing wrong in doing so. I have listened to Christian ministers tell jokes that must stagger the angels—and these preachers seemed to see nothing wrong in it. When Miriam, Moses' sister, objected to his wife Zipporah—who was black, a Cushite (from Ethiopia)—the slur was almost certainly racial. God intervened and struck Miriam with leprosy (Numbers 12:1–11), which makes a person almost whiter than white! Some surmise that

God sent a message to Miriam as if to say, "If you think being white is better, I will really make you white!"

We should not have to wait until we get to heaven to discover how much God hates racism and being racially prejudiced. Christians who should take the lead have often lagged behind. I do not know how or when God will do it, but count on this: "Every valley shall be raised up, every mountain and hill made low; the rough ground shall become level, the rugged places a plain" (Isaiah 40:4). God will roll up His sleeves and judge those who have fancied that the color of their skin makes them a cut above others.

I teach that when it comes to total forgiveness, those who have been hurt the most have the greatest potential blessing—if they totally forgive those who were unjust. This tells me that a lot of black Christians, if they will follow through with this teaching (as I have seen many do as I have preached all over the world), will receive incalculable blessing. How marvelous if those who have been the most hurt will lead the way in total forgiveness—whether in South Africa or Alabama or Pakistan.

I would like to address black Christians who read these lines. If you live in a place like South Africa or in certain parts of America, you have probably been stigmatized because of the color of your skin. On top of that you have confessed Jesus Christ as your Lord and Savior. That means a double stigma. But God knows your name, your address, your background, your hurt and what they have said to you. If you find grace not to retort or get even, God will step in for you one of these days—and it will be worth waiting for. The sad thing is, so much racial injustice has been perpetrated by those who call themselves Christian—especially in America's Deep South.

When I was in Durban, South Africa, I could not help but remember that this was the city where Mahatma Ghandi lived for a while, and seriously considered Christianity. He rejected that option when he witnessed the blatant racism of South African white Christians. I am amazed that Nelson Mandela, who suffered more at the hands of white Christians than nearly anybody reading this book, could still call himself a Methodist and a Christian. I am amazed that many black people in the Deep South of America became Christians.

Some of our best worship singing has sprung from the suffering of black Christians. Marian Anderson, the African-American contralto, was refused a booking to sing at DAR (Daughters of the American Revolution) Constitution Hall in Washington, D.C., in 1939 because she was black. Eleanor Roosevelt, wife of President Franklin Roosevelt, resigned from the DAR in protest, and famously arranged for Anderson to sing at the Lincoln Memorial. Years later the contralto was invited to sing at Constitution Hall, and I was privileged to be there. The ovation was historic and thrilling. She sang many spirituals. The one I fell most in love with, which I had not heard before, was this:

> I told Jesus it would be all right if He changed my
> name, changed my name.
> Jesus told me I would have to live humble if He changed
> my name, changed my name.
> Jesus told me I would have to suffer if He changed my
> name, changed my name.
> I told Jesus it would be all right if He changed my
> name, changed my name.

Many readers will not have to overcome the double stigma of being both black and Christian in a white society. But those who have this inheritance have a promise of blessing greater than offered to me, for I have not suffered as they have. And whether you are red, yellow, black or white and are a follower of Jesus Christ, welcome any stigma if it is because of your obedience to Christ—whenever it comes and from whomever it comes—for when you get called a name you do not like because of your faith, you have an opportunity to glorify your Lord Jesus Christ. Take that stigma with both hands.

I have never been very happy that some (not all) Jewish people who have come to accept Jesus as their Messiah seem to resent the name *Christian*. It's sadly true. They want to be called followers of Yeshua—or Messianic Jews. The name *Christian* therefore carries a stigma with some of them. I can understand this—you only need to consider that Martin Luther was anti-Semetic and how the Holocaust was brought on by so-called Christians. I also understand that these Messianic Jews want to reach fellow Jews with as little offense as possible, hoping to remove any unnecessary impediment. But the Scripture is still true, and I lovingly plead with them that if we suffer as a "Christian" we should not be ashamed but rather "praise God that you bear that name," that name being "Christian." I urge you not to be ashamed of that Name.

Have you ever been called a "holy roller"? I have, in my youth, although I did not deserve it. When Nazarenes back in my old church in Ashland, Kentucky, were called "Noisyrenes," because they could be heard a mile away, they assumed we were rolling in the aisles inside. But I Googled "holy roller" and found that the term is associated with Pentecostals or those who go to a "charismatic church." Nazarenes were neither Pentecostal nor charismatic, and I cannot recall anybody rolling on the floor in my old church. I could easily imagine it happening at Cane Ridge years before. As for rolling on the floor, I have not done this (yet), but I sometimes envy those who did. Not because I want to get called "holy roller" but because these people rolled on the floor for a good reason—they were so full of joy that they momentarily forgot to care about how they appeared. Those on the outside looking in needed to give them a nickname. Holy Roller worked pretty well.

When we get to heaven, we will have no carnal pride such as worrying about our reputation and what we are called. What if it turned out that the more ignoble names you are called because you are a follower of Jesus, the greater your reward in heaven? Would you mind being called "holy roller," "charismatic," "holy Joe," "tongues speaker," "born again," "practicing Christian"— or plain old "Christian"—if you found out this added to your reward in heaven? Well, guess what—*it does*. If you take it with dignity and see it as a privilege, that is. I will not get a "Well done" from Jesus for being called a "no-label man," though this is my favorite appellation here below. But if I get referred to in a negative way—whether it be their chosen nickname for me or sheer lies—and I do not hit back, God looks forward to that day more than I do when He can say to me, "Well done." The bliss, the joy, the euphoria will be so great that I will need a glorified body to take it in!

They say in Hollywood, "Call me anything, just spell my name right." They used to say in Kentucky, "Call me anything but don't call me late for dinner." I say, "Call me anything if it is connected to my efforts to follow the Lord Jesus Christ."

7

THE UNNECESSARY SCANDAL

If you suffer, it should not be as a murderer or thief or any other kind of criminal, or even as a meddler.

— 1 Peter 4:15

Do not give dogs what is sacred; do not throw your pearls to pigs. If you do, they may trample them under their feet, and then turn and tear you to pieces.

— Matthew 7:6

When my family and I were on vacation in America during the time I was at Westminster Chapel, the four of us were excited to be driving behind a car with a bumper sticker that said, "Honk if you love Jesus." You never see that in England. So I honked. The driver of the car rolled down the car window and shook his fist in the air, clearly annoyed that I honked at him. I assured him that I only honked because of the bumper sticker, believing it to be a serious invitation. I was wrong and the driver of the car had apparently forgotten about his bumper sticker. My guess is, the bumper sticker probably offends a lot of people and my honking certainly offended that driver. Nobody was better off.

That is the way it is with some stigmas. Even though some offenses are supposedly rooted in what is called "Christian," and these people intend to "spread the word"—even via bumper stickers—such people can do more harm than good. That is also the way it is with an unnecessary stigma. It is certainly possible to cause a needless offense. One summer, my dad let us use his car to drive around America. We were embarrassed for a whole month by his bumper sticker, "In case of the Rapture, this car will self-destruct." I decided to Google "Jesus bumper stickers" and found more than I cared to know about: *Jesus saves, Obama spends; Jesus is my airbag; Real men love Jesus; Got Jesus?; Go, Jesus! It's yer birthday; I bet Jesus would have used His turn signals; Are you following Jesus this close?* "Stigmas" like these bumper stickers make me cry out, "Oh, to be living in England again!" You can understand J. I. Packer's observation that America's Bible Belt is a thousand miles wide and one inch deep! So much of Christianity is more cultural than scriptural and for those of us who want to inject a measure of theological sanity into the scene, we have our work cut out.

† MORE THAN ONE THING CAN OFFEND

If I offend anybody I pray it will only be because of the sheer word of God in an atmosphere of love—the Gospel, the person and work of Jesus Christ and all that encourages true godliness. I do not like to offend at all, but if I do cause offense I do not want it to be because of my weird personality, my eccentric habits, my foolish points of view that have nothing to do with sound theology, my unguarded comments in the pulpit, my political opinions, the color of my shirt, my insensitive comments to you or about your lifestyle or my being nosy regarding your personal life.

† THE WEAK AND STRONG

There are perhaps two types of people within the scope of the Christian family whom you should be concerned not to offend: those who are weak and those who are strong. Those who were weak in Paul's day included those who could not eat meat that had been sacrificed to an idol, even though doing so was harmless (1 Corinthians 8:4–8). He warned those who could eat meat with a good conscience nonetheless to be careful "that the exercise of your rights does not become a stumbling block to the weak" (1 Corinthians 8:9). They could needlessly offend a sincere believer and even destroy them (Romans 14:15). There would be Christians nowadays who would take offense if you attended a cinema or drank a glass of wine. You might hope to explore with them whether such restrictions are truly necessary. And yet you should guard against bringing about a needless stigma.

But those who are strong can, rightly or wrongly, get offended, too. I know some who fancy they are "strong" but are nonetheless offended because of other Christians who are teetotalers, impatiently thinking they should grow up. If we are truly strong, surely we will be patient with people like that. On the other hand, I know of someone called Frankie who was horrified when his mother turned down an offer of wine in Italy, saying to the perplexed waiter, "No, we're Christians." It almost turned Frankie against Christianity. And yet some of us who think we are strong and seasoned Christians can be sadly impatient with those who are not very knowledgeable of the Bible. If we are truly mature we should be all the more gentle and understanding and not get offended with those who have not developed theologically as we might wish. Showing displeasure with slower Christians causes an unnecessary offense.

Here is a story that I hope will make you smile. Dr. Martyn Lloyd-Jones told me about a week that he and his wife spent with some friends in White Sulphur Springs, West Virginia. The two couples took their meals together for about a week, but their host could not finish a meal without referring to "those so-called Christians who smoke and drink." This man clearly took offense at people like that. The Lloyd-Joneses tried to be gracious without committing themselves, but were rather glad when the week was over. From there they went to Grand Rapids, Michigan. The man who met them at the airport was smoking a cigar, and when they got to his home he invited Dr. Lloyd-Jones to have a whiskey. Martyn was intrigued by the stark difference in cultures between the man in West Virginia and the man in Michigan. But that is not the end of the story. On the following Sunday night, following the church service, as they drove home

Dr. Lloyd-Jones said, "Oh look, there is a Howard Johnson's restaurant—I do love their ice cream." Silence. But the host drove into the restaurant parking lot and they went in. Silence. Dr. Lloyd-Jones spoke: "Is something wrong?" "No, not at all," said the host. "But there must be. You have gone quiet since we have come in—please tell me what is going on." "Well," the man replied, "it is Sunday—the Sabbath—and we never buy on the Sabbath." So the man who smoked cigars and drank whiskey would have offended the West Virginian, but was now offended himself because of Dr. Lloyd-Jones wanting ice cream at a restaurant on a Sunday. When the Lloyd-Joneses returned to their room, Martyn said to his wife, "Everybody seems to have something they are against to feel a bit righteous; I wonder what it is with us—there must be something!"

These are genuine offenses but have nothing to do with the stigma of being a Christian.

† NEEDLESS OFFENSE BY IMBALANCE OF TRUTH

I knew an able minister who had strong Reformed theological views that governed much of his interpretation of Scripture. The trouble was, virtually every sermon he preached was out to prove his theology of man's spiritual inability, predestination and election. I ordered twenty of his sermons. Even though they all have different titles based upon a wide variety of texts, every single one of them is about man's total depravity, election and God's effectual calling or preserving grace to keep people from being lost. I hardly disagreed with a word in those sermons, but I would not send those tapes to most people I know—they needlessly offend.

When I approached this preacher, sadly, he said simply but dogmatically that my problem was that I was offended by the

Gospel—I was put off by the truth. He would say I wanted to avoid the stigma of Christ's work on the cross and that I was only afraid of what people would think. But it always seemed to me that what he did not want to face was that he largely influenced only the narrow group who were already convinced of his teaching and that he actually reached very few people outside his little circle because of this attitude and his inability to accept any criticism. His actual preaching possibly did more harm than good if it was truly the Gospel he was hoping to make known! A strong devotee of C. H. Spurgeon, he thought he was upholding the stigma of Spurgeon's Gospel but in fact he created his own unnecessary offense. I am afraid he was no Spurgeon (who, after all, was so balanced). The stigma he thought he was upholding was certainly offensive but in fact his preaching was cold, dry and doctrinal; there was no sense of it conveying the person of Jesus. It largely put off people from receiving the very Gospel he wanted people to hear. "Perfectly orthodox, perfectly useless," Dr. Lloyd-Jones would say.

I knew this Reformed minister very well. I had long wished I could share something with him that, in my opinion, would have enriched him. It had to do with his being more loving, more open to the Holy Spirit, being more evangelistic and witnessing to everybody. But I also know that when I tried to share with him some of the precious things that happened to me, it would be an example of wasting precious truths. So much so that I felt it was not unlike Jesus warning us not to cast our pearls before pigs (Matthew 7:6). When Jesus said we should not cast our pearls before pigs, it was only a figure of speech, meaning not to waste precious truths upon those who will not only be unappreciative but will vehemently attack us for our efforts to share with them.

The first person I baptized at Westminster Chapel was a Los Angeles Jew and international businessman named Jay Michaels.

He became a dear friend, though he is now in heaven. He was converted at the chapel but needed a church in California. I recommended what I thought was a good church for him. Jay introduced himself to the pastor and told him I had recommended the church to him. You would have thought the pastor would rejoice in the conversion of this businessman. But the pastor immediately said to Jay, "R. T. Kendall does not believe in limited atonement." Jay had no idea what the pastor was talking about. It was a case of the pastor causing needless offense, all because a debatable point of doctrine was too important to him. This pastor unnecessarily offended not only a weaker brother but a brand-new Christian.

Casting our pearls before pigs can include prematurely dishing out doctrine that people cannot possibly take in. We can so easily offend good people with "true truth" (to use Francis Schaeffer's term) for which they are not yet ready. We must be sure that what we teach is what people are able to receive and that, most of all, it is the Gospel that offends and not our private interpretations on issues that are not essential.

† SUFFERING FOR THE WRONG REASONS

I know of able ministers who are now sidelined because of their indiscretions, whether regarding money or sex. Their being out of the ministry is painful for them. Some have taken their being disciplined by their ecclesiastical authorities with dignity; others were indignant and demanded to return almost immediately. There is a stigma associated with preaching the Gospel—and nobody should be sidelined for this kind of offense. But when we bring disgrace upon the Name of Christ generally, we should take the punishment. This is why Peter said, "If you suffer, it should not be as a murderer or thief or any other kind of criminal, or even as a meddler" (1 Peter 4:15). In other words, do not suffer because of committing *sin*.

Let's be fair, honest and candid. We have all suffered because of our sinful mistakes. I have. You probably have, too. We pay dearly for it—and so we should. But whom the Lord loves He chastens, or disciplines, all because we belong to Him (Hebrews 12:6). God disciplines us that we might partake of His holiness (Hebrews 12:10). I have written a book called *Second Chance*. I believe fallen Christians, including ministers, can be forgiven and restored—and be used again. Whereas God's forgiveness can be immediate—God is gracious (1 John 1:9)—the restoration takes time. People who disgrace the Church by scandalous behavior should not be allowed back too soon.

✝ MEDDLING

God wants true holiness to characterize His servants. His chastening is to bring us to holiness. "God disciplines us for our good, in order that we may share in his holiness" (Hebrews 12:10). Paul said, "But among you there must not be even a hint of sexual immorality" (Ephesians 5:3). The world loves it when there is sexual scandal in the church. The world will leap at the chance to focus on any minister who has a history of sexual misconduct.

Peter adds that we should not even suffer as a "meddler"—a "busybody" (KJV). That means being nosy. Trying to sort things out when it is outside our responsibility to do so. Asking questions when it is none of our business. Trying to get involved in people's lives when they ask us to stay away. Intruding where we are not welcome. Those of us who do this sort of thing end up with egg on our faces. We cause needless offense. It is not the Gospel and its intrinsic stigma at stake but our lack of wisdom.

A meddling lady came up to a man who was standing in a line with his child at a camp meeting, waiting for their food. She said to him, "The Lord told me that your daughter should not be wearing trousers but should be wearing a skirt." The man replied, "If the Lord really told you that, He would have revealed that this is my son—who needs a haircut." The poor lady was very embarrassed—but had given, and suffered, a needless rebuke.

I have a lot of friends who are known as charismatics. I preach for them all the time (which causes some evangelicals to be a bit skeptical of me). Some of them, however, have done their own cause a disservice by accusing evangelicals of not having the Holy Spirit—or not being very spiritual—because they do not speak in tongues. Big mistake. This, too, is meddling, doing more harm than good. Paul says all Christians have the Holy Spirit (Romans 8:9), that we could not confess Christ as Lord apart from the Holy Spirit (1 Corinthians 12:3). Not only that, when Paul asked the question, "Do all speak in tongues?" (1 Corinthians 12:30), the answer is obviously no. There is enough stigma regarding the Holy Spirit in any case—as I will show below—without having to push a certain agenda that makes many people who love the Lord feel spiritually inferior—and rejected. Pushing speaking in tongues often causes unnecessary offense to very godly people. The most godly man I ever knew—my own dad—never spoke in tongues.

† TAKING TO THE STREETS

My second sermon was preached when I was nineteen. It was on Broadway Street in Nashville in December 1954. In those days it was legal to have street meetings. A group from Trevecca Nazarene University sang hymns and songs just before I went to the microphone to preach on the text, "Is it nothing to you, all ye that pass by?" (Lamentations 1:12, KJV). I think we should take seriously the verse, "By all means save some" (1 Corinthians 9:22). I have therefore felt a certain sympathy for those preachers on street corners who preach the Gospel to passers-by. But I have to admit I do cringe when I hear some of them. There was a man in Headington, Oxford, where we lived for three years, who would shout at those of us who got off the bus each evening—preaching the Gospel (I listened carefully to him to check). I wanted to speak to him and wish him well—and did. But I feared, too, he was not helping the cause very much.

What worked many years ago does not always work today. George Whitefield left the ornate pulpits of the Church of England and went to the fields in the eighteenth century—and reached—and converted—thousands. John Wesley criticized Whitefield for this but eventually followed him—and reached—and converted—thousands. This practice does not work very well today. When we first followed Arthur Blessitt into the streets, he actually tried preaching at Victoria Station—and was doing brilliantly, but a policeman made him stop. As I mentioned earlier, our Pilot Lights took to the streets between Buckingham Palace and Victoria Street and it is a ministry that is still going strong, but our ministry was giving out pamphlets and engaging in conversations. The day may come when this, too, will be forbidden. I would say that it is a legitimate stigma when it is legal to do so. We have received countless accounts of people who have come to Christ through this ministry. But if the law changes and forbids ministry such as what the Pilot Lights do, it could be bringing an unnecessary stigma on the Church to carry on.

† LET IT BE THE GOSPEL THAT OFFENDS

As I write these lines, I am 74. I do not know how long God will let me live. I only know that I want to end well. When I hear of people's lack of wisdom or falling into sin, I say in my heart, "That's me—but by the grace of God." I do not want to bring about an offense—whether regarding money, sex or power—or lack of wisdom. But I do not mind offending for the Gospel. That is a stigma I will accept. I only pray that it will be the Gospel—and nothing else—that causes offense if it must come.

8

OUT ON A LIMB

You, however, know all about my teaching, my way of life, my purpose, faith.

— *2 Timothy 3:10*

You are in error because you do not know the Scriptures or the power of God.

— *Matthew 22:29*

There are some things I believe that I would not go to the stake for. Take ecclesiology (that is, church issues), for example. The New Testament actually presents three different forms of church government: congregational, presbyterian and episcopal. I would uphold the congregational position, but I would not die for this. I could list many points of view I hold that are important but not essential. There are perhaps some who would make a stigma out of their ecclesiology, but I wouldn't.

To me the true stigma pertains almost entirely to things soteriological (that is, the doctrine of salvation). There are certain soteriological positions I would die for—but with which not all my friends agree. I myself, however, would go to the stake for what I will espouse in this chapter. The stigma I may suffer for these doctrinal views is therefore something I myself have accepted, but I am not for one minute intending to impose my beliefs on you! But I wanted nonetheless to have a section in this book that shows some of the things I have held to and—in some cases—have been stigmatized for. You can decide down the road to what extent you would take these teachings on board. I could easily write a whole book on each of these points, so please understand that I will be necessarily brief in order to summarize these particular issues into one chapter.

† THE FAITH OF CHRIST

This is one of the most precious teachings I have come to discover. Jesus as a man lived by faith in His Father (Hebrews 2:13), but His faith, unlike ours, was a perfect faith: He had the Holy Spirit without any limit (John 3:34). You and I have a limit, or measure, of faith (Romans 12:3), but Jesus had a perfect faith.

Why is this important? It was foundational to Paul's own understanding of justification by faith. The righteousness of God, said Paul, is revealed "from faith to faith," as the King James Version puts it (Gr. *ek pisteos eis pistiv*). There are times when I want to use only the King James Version, and this is one of those times! This is when I have to work doubly hard if using a modern version. I regret that modern versions often gloss over and reinterpret rather than literally translate when it comes to some very important passages. So what does "faith to faith" mean? "Faith to faith" means *Jesus' faith and our faith;* His perfect faith must be ratified by our faith. This is why Paul went on to say, "Even the righteousness of God which is by *faith of Jesus Christ* [Gr. *pisteos Ieusou Christou*] unto all and *upon all them that believe*" (Romans 3:22, KJV, emphasis mine). Jesus believed perfectly, but if you and I do not also believe, there will be no righteousness put to our credit. His faith is only efficacious for "all them that believe."

Paul said exactly the same thing in Galatians: A man is justified "by the faith of Jesus Christ [Gr. *dia pisteos Iesou Christou*], even we have believed *in Jesus Christ* [Gr. *eis Christon Iesouv*], that we might be justified *by the faith of* Christ" [Gr. *ina dikaiosthomen ek pisteos Christou*, lit. "in order that we might be justified from faith of Christ"] (Galatians 2:16, KJV, emphasis mine). Paul is teaching that we are actually justified by Christ's own faith as long as we, too, believe. This is why he uses the purpose clause "in order that." His point: Christ's faith is the meritorious cause of our justification; our faith is the instrumental cause.

This then is why he uses the expression "faith to faith": Christ's faith is of no value to us unless we also believe. Paul has so carefully worded this; we have believed "in" Christ in order that we might be justified "by the faith of Christ." It is Christ's *obedience*—His perfect faith that enabled Him to produce the sinless life and obedient death—that Paul is trusting in (Romans 5:19). This is part of the reason Paul also says that we are "saved through his life!" The *whole* of His life—from Jesus' birth to His burial, even His resurrection and ascension—is the ground of our justification (Romans 5:10). But on one condition: You and I must believe as well.

Paul summarized this when he said in Galatians 2:20 (KJV), "I live by the faith of the Son of God" (Gr. *en pistei zo ti tou viou tou theou,* lit. "In faith I live by that of the Son of God"). In other words, Paul is not only justified by the faith of Christ but *lives* by the faith of Christ as well. By the way, it is a wonderful way to live! It means relying on Him all the time.

All this is demonstrated by the context of Habakkuk 2:4, quoted three times in the New Testament (Romans 1:17; Galatians 3:11; Hebrews 10:38) but from the Septuagint (the Greek translation of the Old Testament), which says, "The just shall live by faith." But the Hebrew reads, "The righteous shall live by his faithfulness," meaning *God's* faithfulness. The context proves it is God's faithfulness that we live by, as Habakkuk was told to wait for the revelation: "Though it linger, wait for it" (Habakkuk 2:3). We trust God to be faithful since He is the one who promised it. Indeed, these are the exact words in Hebrews: "He who promised is faithful" (Hebrews 10:23) and, "He who is coming will come and will not delay" (Hebrews 10:37); hence the righteous will live by God's faithfulness. I myself would be fearful of living by my own faith or faithfulness, which can vacillate so much. But I am not fearful when it comes to God's unwavering faithfulness. The bottom line: It is not our faith that saves but only our faith in a great Savior!

When our faith is joined by Christ's faith, God puts His righteousness to our credit. We are thus saved not by our righteousness but Christ's, which is transferred to our account as though it were our own. For this reason, we are no more righteous ten years—or fifty years—after our conversion than we were the first day. This is because Christ's righteousness is unimprovable. Thus we can sing,

> My hope is built on nothing less than Jesus' blood and
> righteousness;
> I dare not trust the sweetest frame but wholly lean on
> Jesus' name.
> On Christ the solid Rock I stand, all other ground is
> sinking sand,
> All other ground is sinking sand.
>
> — *Edward Mote, 1797–1874*

† ONCE SAVED, ALWAYS SAVED

I have not always believed in "once saved, always saved." Indeed, I was brought up to believe the opposite, even being taught back in Ashland, Kentucky, that the doctrine of eternal security was "born in hell." Two things together changed my mind. First, an immediate witness of the Holy Spirit that came to me on October 31, 1955. I can only say that I knew on that day that I was eternally saved, *no matter what I did*. My friends at Trevecca all predicted I would change my mind. I knew then that I would not—more than 55 years ago. I haven't. The witness was, if anything, more real than people around me. That assurance was as real to me as seeing the blue sky, the trees, the flowers and all my friends. I never knew such assurance was possible.

I may have shocked you when I said *no matter what I did*. I need to tell you that this did not mean I intended to sin as I pleased. That thought never crossed my mind. But it was comforting to me to know that I was saved unconditionally. As long as my salvation depended on my obedience, I could *never know for sure* that I would be in heaven one day. But that experience in 1955 was virtually like going to heaven and back, and I knew beyond any doubt that I would be in heaven one day.

The second thing that convinced me of this doctrine's truth is that this could not be true only of me—but must hold for *all* who trusted Christ alone. It would be unfair for me to say, "I know *I* am eternally saved—but this was for me only." That would be unfair and necessarily untrue. I knew that what was true of me must be true of all who rely on Christ alone, even if they did not receive the infallible assurance I was given. Why I was given this assurance, having never believed in this teaching, I still do not know. But it is not only called full assurance of faith (Hebrews 10:22) but also full assurance of understanding (Colossians 2:2); the Greek word in both places is *plerophoria*—"full assurance." You may have, should God give it, full assurance of your salvation but also understanding of doctrine. I do not have *plerophoria* of all I hold to—e.g., ecclesiology (as I said above). But what I write about in this section is what I would die for because I am so totally convinced of these things.

A couple of years before we left London I was at a party when a man came up to me and said, "So you are R. T. Kendall who wrote the book *Once Saved, Always Saved?* I don't agree with that book." "Then you have read it?" I asked. "No," he replied, "but I know that it isn't true." Then he said to me, "Give me your best shot—you have two minutes, convince me." Although I thought that was a bit unfair, I said, "Okay, here goes," and as I did with him I will now share with you only one biblical reason I hold to this teaching. That is the New Testament teaching of adoption. This doctrine implicitly shows God's election as well. When we are adopted into God's family, it is His choice, not ours. We did not *ask* to be adopted—God adopted us. But once we are adopted into the family we are declared "children of God." We are all sons and daughters of God. If I may put it this way, Jesus is God's only "natural" Son, being the eternally begotten Word of God who was in the beginning with God and was God (John 1:1). And yet we, too, are children of God. But there is more: How secure do you suppose Jesus Himself is in the Godhead? Is there any possibility that Jesus could be disenfranchised by the Father and put out of the Trinity? No. It is unthinkable. And yet we are called joint-heirs, co-heirs with Jesus (Romans 8:17), which is the reason Paul uses the phrase "in Christ" many times! We, then, are as secure *in Christ* as Christ Himself is secure in the Trinity. That, if you ask me, is pretty secure.

At the natural level, in any court, when a child is adopted by parents, that child is given all the rights of a natural-born son or daughter. I can never forget hearing a judge say soberly to a young couple who petitioned the court to adopt a son: "When I sign my name to this paper, your son becomes legally yours. No court in the land will overturn this document. Your son has all the protection of the state as if he were your own child. There is nothing you can do to change this once I sign my name to this document. I must tell you: Your child could cost you a fortune if he becomes ill; he may disappoint you if he turns to drugs, but he is your son forever—from the moment I sign this paper. Do you understand this? Do you want me to sign it?" The couple said gladly to the judge, "Sign it."

I told that story to the man at the party. He said he would think about it. By the way, I did not write the book *Once Saved, Always Saved* to convince people who did not believe it but to assure those who wanted to believe it but were afraid the teaching wasn't true. *It is true!*

† THE PLACE OF WORKS

Paul said we are saved by grace through faith—"not by works, so that no one can boast" (Ephesians 2:8–9). He went on to say that we are God's workmanship, created in Christ Jesus "to do good works" (Ephesians 2:10). Those works are not what saves us, however; the works show that God has done a sovereign work in us and we are put on our honor to maintain good works as *gratitude* to God for such a wonderful gift. Good works, or sanctification, show our gratitude to God.

But what if those good works are absent? Can good works be absent in a true believer? I reply: Not entirely, but we can still be lax in showing good works. Otherwise Paul would not urge us to show good works! We need to be reminded, encouraged and warned. And yet it is a fair question: What if good works are relatively absent in us? I will give three possibilities.

James's View of Faith and Works

First, if we do not show good works, we will not influence those around us who need what we have. For one thing, we will have no influence on the poor man out there, who will be unimpressed by our faith if we do not also show care for him. James raised the question, "If someone says he has faith but does not have works? Can that faith save him?" (James 2:14, ESV). The *him* (accusative, masculine, singular) referred to the poor man in James 2:6, when James said, "You have dishonored the 'poor man,'" as in the English Standard Version (Gr. *protochon*—accusative, masculine, singular). People (including Martin Luther) hastily assume that James changed the subject from the poor man in James 2:6 to a different "him" in verse 14. But there is an alternate I should like to propose. He has not changed the subject but is still discussing the same poor man. When you understand this, the rest of the chapter reads by itself. There is not the slightest variance between Paul and James. In a word, if our works do not match our faith we are not going to save the poor man out there. The world wants to see works in us that make our faith attractive. But, sadly, sometimes Christians forget this and do not make a good impression on the world. This does not, however, mean that such Christians are not saved. We have all failed here. The "him" of James 2:14 refers to the poor man of James 2:6. He will be unimpressed if we do not bless him by good deeds, says James (James 2:15–18).

1 Corinthians 3:15

Second, if we do not demonstrate good works then, sadly, we will build a superstructure of wood, hay or straw and these will be burned up on the Day of Christ (1 Corinthians 3:12–15). The foundation is Jesus Christ (1 Corinthians 3:11), but we must build on that foundation a superstructure that will not dissolve in the fire at the judgment seat of Christ. This means we must take care to erect a superstructure of gold, silver and precious stones—which will not burn up in the fire of God's final judgment.

When we walk in the light, obey His Word in everything, totally forgive our enemies and show gratitude to God by our attitude, we build a superstructure of gold, silver and precious gems. But on the other hand, not glorifying Christ by godliness, faithfulness and obedience means erecting a superstructure of wood, hay or straw. You can build such a vulnerable superstructure by not walking in the light, carelessness, holding grudges, complaining all the time and not being like Jesus. Sin not repented of makes a superstructure of wood, hay or straw.

Those who are on the foundation are saved. But those who build a superstructure of wood, hay or straw will have their works "burned up." Such a person "will suffer loss," namely, they will receive no reward. All who are saved will go to heaven, but not all who go to heaven will receive a reward at the judgment seat of Christ.

> If what has been built survives [gold, silver, precious gems], the builder will receive a reward. If it is burned up, the builder will suffer loss but yet will be saved—even though only as one escaping through the flames.
>
> — *1 Corinthians 3:14–15*

Hebrews 6:4–6, a Difficult Passage

Third, if you do not maintain good works you will cease to hear the voice of God—and will be rendered incapable of repenting—ever again. This is the meaning of one of the more difficult passages in the Bible. Hebrews 6:4–6 is not a favorite of most Calvinists and Arminians. Calvinists are often threatened by this passage since they teach that a Christian cannot fall away (this passage says in the Greek they already did); Arminians teach that if you do fall away you can come back again (this passage says you can't). This text does not refer to losing your salvation but the ability to hear God speak. Samson, who did come back after a great fall, obviously could still hear God speak to him.

The key to grasping this passage is in Hebrews 5:11, where the writer says these Hebrew Christians had become "dull of hearing" (KJV), which means "hard of hearing." The writer earlier quoted from Psalm 95, warning, "If you hear his voice, do not harden your hearts" (Hebrews 3:15). As long as you can hear God speak, good! But if you get spiritually hard of hearing, you will find it more and more difficult to hear God speak. The worst scenario is being stone-deaf, when you cannot hear at all. That is what happened to some of those Hebrew Christians.

Those described in Hebrews 6:4–6 are truly saved people. Their having fallen away was not a fall from salvation but falling from communion with God. It was because they did not listen to God and eventually became stone-deaf. The reference that they could not be renewed again—or brought back to repentance—was so worded because they had indeed repented at one time. But something went wrong and they could no longer hear God's voice, nor would they ever. This is so sad. It can happen to any of us. If we do not maintain a close walk with God and keep intimacy with Him, we will cease to hear Him. Do not let that happen! If it does, says the writer of Hebrews, you will not be able to repent—ever again. This repentance is the same thing as being changed from glory to glory (2 Corinthians 3:18, KJV). But that will stop forever if we reach a point where we follow in the steps of the ancient children of Israel in the desert when God swore in His wrath they would never enter the promised land—a euphemism not for heaven but inheriting things that "have to do with salvation," including their inheritance (Hebrews 6:9–12).

Works do not save us but the absence of them has serious consequences—our failure to win the lost, especially the poor man, our failure to receive a reward at the judgment seat of Christ and our failure to hear God speak again. But thank God that we are not saved by works. For if that were the case, who would be saved?

† THE WORD AND SPIRIT

For a long time I have taken the view that there has been a silent divorce in the Church, speaking generally, between the Word and the Spirit. When there is a divorce, sometimes the children stay with the mother, sometimes with the father. In this divorce I now speak of there are those on the "Word" side and those on the "Spirit" side.

What is the difference? Take those on the Word side: What is their emphasis? "We need to get back to expository preaching, earnestly contending for the faith once delivered to the saints, to uphold the doctrines rediscovered by the Reformers—justification by faith, salvation by grace alone, sovereignty of God. Until these truths are recovered and faithfully preached in our generation the honor of God's Name will not be restored." What is wrong with that emphasis? Nothing, in my opinion: What they are saying is exactly right.

Take those on the Spirit side: What is their emphasis? "We need to get back to the book of Acts where there were signs, wonders and miracles—where lying to the Spirit resulted in instant death, praying resulted in the place being shaken, walking in Peter's shadow resulted in people being healed and delivered, where the gifts of the Spirit were in operation. Until we see a demonstration of the Holy Spirit like this the honor of God's Name will not be restored."

What is wrong with that emphasis? Nothing, in my opinion: This emphasis is exactly right.

Until there is a coming together of the Word and Spirit, revival will be delayed, churches will continue to be irrelevant to the world and people generally will not grow in faith or have a burden for the lost.

Jesus said to the Sadducees, "You do not know the Scriptures or the power of God" (Matthew 22:29). What a put-down to them! Jesus flatly told them their problem was that of ignorance; they knew neither the Scriptures nor the power of God. The Sadducees felt they knew the Scriptures backward and forward. As for the power of God, this did not interest them in the slightest. In any case, said Jesus, they were ignorant of these two things.

The problem in the Church today, as I see it, is that it is not a matter of being ignorant of both but rather being divided between those who emphasize one or the other. Both sides seem to dig in their heels and will not admit to a serious problem. Those known as evangelicals fancy that they know their Bibles, understand sound orthodoxy and uphold what is good teaching more than anybody. Their problem is further identified, to quote Jack Taylor, in their probable doctrine of the Trinity: God the Father, God the Son and God the Holy Bible. Some look at Charismatics or Pentecostals as the lunatic fringe of Christianity and refuse to learn a single thing from them. "Of course we believe in the Holy Spirit," they say. They have virtually no concept of the immediate and direct witness of the Holy Spirit, however. Their emphasis is on the fruits of the Spirit rather than the gifts.

Some argue that you cannot separate the Word from the Spirit. I know what they mean by that. But the fact that Paul said, "Our gospel came to you not simply with words, but also with power, with the Holy Spirit and deep conviction" (1 Thessalonians 1:5) shows that he *might* have preached the Gospel without having the power all preachers hope for. Indeed, I myself know what it is to preach under the anointing of the Spirit and I know equally what it is to preach with little or no power at all. Paul, however, could say it again, "My message and my preaching were not with wise and persuasive words, but with a demonstration of the Spirit's power, so that your faith might not rest on human wisdom, but on God's power" (1 Corinthians 2:4–5).

The problem with charismatics and Pentecostals, it seems to me, is that they reckon they preach nothing but the Bible! "Of course we believe the Bible," say these people. "Don't insult us by suggesting we don't believe the Word of God." They do not see any real problem despite the fact that their theological understanding tends not to be very deep, that worship and lively singing sometimes seem more important to them than the Bible and that their emphasis on the gifts is greater than on the fruits of the Spirit.

I was once invited by John Wimber to have dinner with him and Carol at the Rembrandt Hotel in London. To my surprise—and dismay—I felt I had a "word" for John. It so troubled me that

I decided to fast for the entire day. When we met, I said, "John, I think I have a word for you." "Shoot," he said. I reminded him of what he had preached on the previous Monday at the Royal Albert Hall, that "Luther and Calvin gave us the Word in the sixteenth century, we are called to do the works in the twentieth century." I said, "John, you are teaching Pharaohs that knew not Joseph, assuming that the people in the twentieth century know the Word that the Reformers gave the church. You are asking people to do the 'works,' assuming they know the Word because it was given to the church in the sixteenth century; people today don't have a clue what the Reformers taught." He looked at me, pointing to his chest, and said, "You have put your finger on the very heart of where I am in my thinking. I accept your word." Whether it made any difference after that day, I do not know.

The truth is, we need to emphasize the Word and Spirit equally, the gifts as much as the fruits and be as open to the immediate and direct witness of the Spirit as much as knowing sound theology.

The stigma one often bears is to call for *both*, and one is sometimes stigmatized by both Word people on the one side and Spirit people on the other! People want to stay in their comfort zones—and sleep on while the world is on the brink of unprecedented disaster and people are on their way to hell as well. I continue to pray that the Word and Spirit will be remarried, believing that the simultaneous combination will result in spontaneous combustion.

When I was at Westminster Chapel, I would frequently get the comment following a sermon, "Thank you for your word." That was what they came for, that is what they got. They did not expect to *see* anything—a miracle or sign or wonder; they only expected to hear. And I suppose there are churches where people go to see things; they do not expect to *hear* very much—such as delving into historical or expositional theology; they go to see. But if we were willing to bear the stigma attaching to a commitment to this simultaneous combination of the Word and Spirit, and if churches would equally *uphold and experience both,* the day would come—may God hasten the day, to quote my friend Lyndon Bowring—that "the people who go to see will hear, and those who go to hear will see."

9

THE REASON THE JEWS MISSED THEIR MESSIAH

How can you believe since you accept glory from one another but do not seek the glory that comes from the only God?

— *John 5:44*

His parents . . . were afraid of the Jewish leaders, who already had decided that anyone who acknowledged that Jesus was the Messiah would be put out of the synagogue.

— *John 9:22*

Some readers may know about my friendship with Rabbi David Rosen, one of Israel's most distinguished Orthodox Jewish rabbis. He was the first Jew to receive a papal knighthood and the first recipient of a papal knighthood from the present Pope Benedict XVI. David and I have written a book, *The Christian and the Pharisee: Two Outspoken Leaders Debate the Way to Heaven*. The title was David's choice. David unashamedly sees himself as a Pharisee. He believes that the New Testament misrepresents Pharisees. The book was launched at Westminster Abbey and has been acclaimed by Jews, evangelical Christians and Messianic Jews. In it, I show why I believe Jesus is Israel's true Messiah and David gives his reasons for believing otherwise. Perhaps the most striking thing about the book is that David and I remained very good friends; indeed, many readers and those who have interviewed us on radio and television have commented that they can tell we are fond of each other. I had hoped to see him truly converted, but that has not happened (yet)! I pray for David daily—that he might be the Saul of Tarsus—of modern Israel—i.e., their apostle Paul.

I have a keen interest in the subject of Israel. I love Israel and have been there many times. I love the Jews and have a passionate desire to see God's historically chosen people turn to God and acknowledge their Messiah—Jesus Christ of Nazareth. I should add that I also love Palestinians. I have also been to Palestine several times, had a friendly relationship with the late President Yasser Arafat (he called me his "only friend" in the West) and still keep in touch with Dr. Saeb Erekat, the Palestinians' chief negotiator with the Israelis.

The word "stigma" pops up everywhere when it comes to the subject of this chapter. I was stigmatized by many for being friendly with Arafat. Some are also offended when I say we should evangelize the Jews (as best we can). Some even call you anti-Semitic if you say anything that suggests that Israel particularly, and Jews generally, have left God out of their agenda, despite the high level of secularization of the State of Israel. It does not seem to matter much to some that America, despite its staunch defense of human rights, nonetheless unquestioningly supports Israel, a nation that will put you in jail if you witness to a Jew in that country about Jesus Christ. So there is a vast and deep stigma around the present subject. The most volatile subject of all is that which pertains to any responsibility the Jews may have had in the crucifixion of Jesus; you are truly anti-Semitic if you suggest they had anything at all to do with it.

What we all know is that the Jews generally failed to accept Jesus as their Messiah. Not all Jews, of course—the first twelve apostles were Jews, Saul of Tarsus was a Jew and so were thousands of early converts—but the majority of the nation. This situation is not permanent. Things will change. One day the Jews—hundreds and hundreds of thousands of them—will openly, gladly and loudly welcome and proclaim Jesus Christ of Nazareth as their Messiah. That day is coming and it is coming soon. But there is, as I write these lines, a "blindness" upon the minds of the people of Israel, speaking generally. As long as this blindness is there, things will not change. But when it is lifted, a multitude that no one will be able to count will receive Jesus Christ as the God-man and as their Lord and Savior. But at the moment these people are spiritually blind; they cannot see the truth because they are blind.

As a matter of fact, when David and I launched our book at Westminster Abbey I explained the reason he does not see the truth about Jesus: It is because of a "double blindness." Why do I say that? First, *all* people are born blind—whether Jews or Gentiles. The "god of this age [Satan] has blinded the minds of unbelievers, so that they cannot see the light of the gospel that displays the glory of Christ, who is the image of God" (2 Corinthians 4:4). The reason *anybody* remains unconverted is due to this blindness upon them which has been inflicted by the devil. But Jews have a blindness on their minds *on top of* the blindness that all people are born with. Paul said, "God gave them [Israel] a spirit of stupor, eyes that could not see and ears that could not hear, to this very day" (Romans 11:8). What some translations call "blindness" (the word I am using) is also translated "hardened," as in the NIV (Romans 11:7, 25). This then is why I say that Jews today have a double blindness on them: what they are born with plus the blindness with which God has inflicted them.

As I said, this will change; the Jews will one day soon accept Jesus Christ as their own Messiah. But I am afraid this is not the book to enlarge further on that. The question is, why did the Jews reject Jesus as their Messiah? This question is important because it is a hint as to how we might somehow penetrate the blindness referred to above.

When Jesus asked the question in John 5:44, "How can you believe since you accept glory from one another but do not seek the glory that comes from the only God?" He revealed then and there the fundamental reason the Jews rejected Jesus. In a word, their love of the praise of people preempted the possibility of faith. "How *can* you believe?" asked Jesus—when what matters to you is not what God thinks but what people think! Jesus put this question to the Jews, almost certainly Pharisees, in John 5 and the whole of that chapter is addressing them. He knew they did not believe in Him. They resented His healing people on the Sabbath, calling God His own Father and making Himself equal with God. They were trying hard at that stage to kill Him. "For this reason [the Jews] tried all the more to kill him" (John 5:18).

What Jesus said to them in John 5:19–43 reaches its climax with this revealing question to them: "How can you believe" when you don't give one jot about the praise that comes from the only God? The KJV says, "Seek not the honour that cometh from God only." The Greek *doxa* may be translated praise, honor or glory, and you find all three words sooner or later when you read various versions. The KJV suggests that there is a praise—honor or glory—that will come from God *alone* . . . if they sought it, if it mattered to them. But whether you translate it "God only" or "only God," the meaning is that these Jews "made no effort" to get the glory God was willing to give them. They had made a choice along the way—who knows when?—to covet, seek, accept, want, desire or wait for praise and honor that comes from *people*. Fancy that! They cared more about what people think than about what God thinks!

This is why when they gave alms they wanted trumpets to sound (Matthew 6:2), when they prayed they made sure people were watching (Matthew 6:5) and when they fasted they would "disfigure their faces to show men they are fasting" (Matthew 6:16). Jesus summed it up: "Everything they do is done for people to see" (Matthew 23:5). They were besotted with wanting admiration and praise from their peers. They lived for it, thrived on it. No wonder, then, says Jesus, they do not believe in their Messiah when He is standing right before their eyes! "How can you believe since you accept glory from one another but *do not seek* the glory that comes from the only God?" It was not on their radar screen to seek the honor God would give. It did not cross their minds to seek His honor.

Should this seeking of the honor of God have occurred to them? Oh yes. Read the Old Testament—the Law, the prophets and the psalms. The honor and glory of God is like a golden thread that is woven through every single page. It was all about God—His will, power, honor, purpose and holiness. But as Stephen testified before the Sanhedrin, "You are just like your ancestors: You always resist the Holy Spirit!" (Acts 7:51). Stephen would agree with every word I am saying in these lines! The Jews of Jesus' day are only repeating the sin of their fathers, forefathers and ancient people who had turned away from the God of glory. Therefore, when the Messiah comes, they are unable to recognize Him.

There wasn't a Pharisee or Sadducee in Israel in Jesus' day who thought that the Messiah would show up and that they would not be the first to recognize Him. "*We'll* know Him, *we'll* know Him," they would not hesitate to say. But they missed Him, following in a spiritual—or I should call it *unspiritual*—succession that had started generations before. But Jesus pronounced a verdict: "Therefore this generation will be held responsible for the blood of all the prophets that has been shed since the beginning of the world" (Luke 11:50). Like it or not, that is what Jesus said.

They did not like Jesus from the first day. They were critical from the start. So, early on it had been decided "that anyone who acknowledged that Jesus was the Messiah would be put out of the synagogue" (John 9:22). That is why the parents of the young man healed of blindness would not say one way or the other what they all knew about their son. They were terrified of being put out of the synagogue.

In the same way the Pharisees were terrified over what their fellow Jews would say if they ever confessed that Jesus was the Messiah. This is why Nicodemus came "at night" to inquire of Jesus (John 3:2). They were as scared as the blind man's parents. They were all afraid. They lived in fear of one another. Therefore, they entirely missed the promised Messiah when He turned up under their noses. That is why Israel missed Him.

I believe all this points a way forward to reach Jews today. If they had hearts to glorify the God of the Bible, God Himself would honor this. That honor would result in the lifting of the blindness on Israel—and they would turn to the Lord (2 Corinthians 3:16). The veil—the inability to see what is there—would be taken away. It would begin with their making every effort to obtain the honor that comes from the only God—the true God, the God of Abraham, Isaac and Jacob. They could read the psalms, for example, with yearning hearts to do God's will. They all could have a serious look at Isaiah 53—and see why their own ancient rabbis saw this as a Messianic prophecy. Psalm 110 would open up to them. All their objections to the Trinity would dissolve once they saw that God sent His one and only Son into the world to die on a cross—and how the cross perfectly fulfilled the Mosaic Law. What Messianic Jews have seen in small numbers, a vast—almost incalculable—number of Jews would see throughout the world! It need not happen only in Jerusalem or Tel Aviv.

In the meantime, we all need to evangelize the world—including Muslims. People asked why I became friendly with Arafat—Israel's sworn enemy. I replied that if envy or jealousy was a fair motive for Paul to reach Jews by seeing Gentiles come to Christ (see Romans 11:11–14), I fancied that winning Yasser Arafat to Christ could have this effect. I certainly tried, as several members of the PLO know very well. My point is this: If Muslims in vast numbers were to come to Jesus Christ, maybe, just maybe, it would provoke Israel in the very direction Paul had in mind. What we do know is that Muslims all over the world are having dreams about Jesus. Arafat told me of a dream he had about Jesus and the Virgin Mary and how it moved him to have a lamb sent to the Church of the Nativity in Bethlehem for the priests there "to have a feast." Many Muslims have these dreams—but they are afraid to talk about them. Our responsibility is to love them. We will not win by argument, in my opinion. They will be won by our *sincere love*. Pray for them and love them. Be kind to them. They need us. Witness to Jews, yes (when you can). But keep reaching out to everybody, praying for Israel the whole time. And if we begin to reach Islamic people, maybe the Jews will wise up—and seek our wisdom.

By the way, who did crucify Jesus? There are at least five answers. First, Pontius Pilate did it. It would not have happened without him, because the Jews had no authority to execute a criminal. Crucifixion was the way they executed criminals in those days and only the Roman governor—Pilate—could make it happen. He did. So blame him (see John 19:1–16). Second, blame the Roman soldiers. They hammered in the nails. They are the ones who scoffed and stripped Jesus and put a scarlet robe on Him, then twisted together a crown of thorns and set it on His head. They mocked Him, "Hail, king of the Jews!" (Matthew 27:27–31). They forced Simon from Cyrene to carry Jesus' cross. "When they [the soldiers] crucified him, they divided up his clothes by casting lots" (Matthew 27:32–35). Third, the Jews cannot avoid their part. It was the high priest and the Sanhedrin that delivered Him to Pilate, asking the governor to crucify Him. Pilate "washed his hands in front of the crowd" and judged himself innocent of Jesus' death and told the Jews it was their responsibility. "All the people answered, "His blood is on us and on our children'!" (Matthew 27:25). Fourth, I did it. Yes, I am the chief culprit. Not the Jews, not the Roman soldiers and not Pontius Pilate. It was *my sins* that led Him to the cross. The crucifixion of Jesus was not an unfortunate martyrdom. It was the reason Jesus came into the world in the first place. He did not die for Himself. He died for us. He who knew no sin was made sin that we might become the righteousness of God in Him (2 Corinthians 5:21). My sins (yours, too) put Jesus on the cross. We are the ones who are guilty. Finally, God did it. The buck stops with Him. He was indeed "stricken by God, smitten by him, and afflicted" (Isaiah 53:4). "It was the LORD's [Yahweh's] will to crush him and cause him to suffer" (Isaiah 53:10). The entire scenario was conceived by God in eternity; the entire proceedings leading up to the death of Jesus Christ were orchestrated from heaven. Jesus was the lamb that was slain from the foundation of the world (1 Peter 1:19–20; Revelation 13:8). Bottom line: God takes the ultimate responsibility for the crucifixion of Jesus.

I am an evangelist. I am a theologian, too, but my heart is to win the lost—wherever they are, whoever they are. All people need Christ or they will be eternally lost. That is the truth, dear friend. You and I have what they need. What they really need. It is Jesus Christ.

One last thing—a word to fellow Christians. As the Jews missed their Messiah because they made no attempt to obtain the honor that comes from the only God, you and I could also miss what God is doing today. Jonathan Edwards taught us that the task of every generation is to discover in which direction the Sovereign Redeemer is moving, then move in that direction. But *how will we know* in which direction the Sovereign Redeemer is moving if we, too, are not seeking the honor that comes from the only true God? If we are more enamored of the praise of people—and more fearful of their ridicule because we avoid the stigma—we, too, will miss what God wants to do in our time.

God is not a respecter of persons. What happened to the Jews—and continues to happen—could happen to us. Do not let that happen.

10

THE STIGMA OF NO VINDICATION

He [God] appeared in a body, was vindicated by the Spirit.

— 1 Timothy 3:16

God is not unjust; he will not forget your work and the love you have shown him as you have helped his people and continue to help them.

— Hebrews 6:10

So do not throw away your confidence; it will be richly rewarded.

— Hebrews 10:35

In 1956 I left Trevecca Nazarene University with no theological degree (I returned to Trevecca to finish later) to enter a ministry with Billy Ball, who had become a mentor. We hoped to see great revival in a series of meetings in a tent that seated two thousand, which we purchased and set up just across the Ohio River from Ashland, Kentucky. That tent was erected behind a huge sign—TRI-STATE EVANGELISTIC CAMPAIGN—which we thought would lead to the revival that would end all revivals. It came to nothing. The peak attendance over some three weeks was fewer than fifty. My dad, who never attended the meetings, was displeased that my future would not be with Nazarenes. He felt I had "broken with God" and wanted assurance that I hadn't. My grandmother, who had bought me a brand new 1955 Chevrolet the year before, took it back—hoping I would wake up. I assured her and my dad that I was following the Lord more closely than ever and that I was going to be used powerfully—even internationally—one day. "Really? When?" my dad asked. "One year from now," I replied, feeling the pressure to come up with something but also being fully convinced that vindication would actually come sooner. I wanted so much to impress my dad and make him feel better.

A year later I was not even in the ministry. I was selling Stroll-o-chairs (as they were called—a type of baby equipment) to couples who were expecting or had just had a baby. I later sold life insurance for two years. Except for being the pastor of a church in Carlisle, Ohio, for eighteen months, which also came to nothing, I worked as a door-to-door vacuum cleaner salesman. For a total of six years I knocked on doors of upper-class homes between Fort Lauderdale and Miami, Florida—selling an expensive vacuum cleaner to people who did not know they needed it until I showed up and persuaded them otherwise. Imagine how proud my dad was of me now! Picture this: people coming to him and asking, "How is your son R. T. these days?" A strained look appeared on his face as he uttered the words, "He works as a door-to-door vacuum cleaner salesman." There is no way you can make that sound very respectable. While my peers from Trevecca were all in full-time ministry, here was I—who had boasted to my father that a worldwide ministry was to be my inheritance in one year—going up to houses all over South Florida as late as 1967, ringing doorbells, and saying, "Hello. I'm R. T. Kendall. I have come to show you something new and different for your home."

It was an embarrassing but memorable time. I cannot say that I was bearing a particular stigma for the Gospel during this time. I must tell you that I had foolishly gone into debt and had to pay my bills before going into full-time ministry. God disciplined me and taught me how to handle money after that. And yet—in spite of this folly—I was doing my best to follow the Lord. I was being prepared for a ministry down the road. It certainly gave me a desire for vindication. In those days I lived for one thing—to be vindicated in order that my dad would see I had not gone off the rails after all. But there was no way I could make selling vacuum cleaners look good when I knew I was supposed to be in a full-time ministry. I learned a lot in those days but perhaps the main thing was that vindication belongs to God, and there is nothing we can do to hasten it. It later became possibly the most dominant theme of my ministry.

† THE MEANING OF VINDICATION

Vindication means having your name cleared from a false accusation. It is to be cleared from blame or suspicion. It is to have the justice of your courage and faith upheld and established by the people who doubted you. We all love to be vindicated. The Jews accused Hebrew Christians of being foolish for professing faith in Jesus of Nazareth. It was embarrassing for them that they had no proof they had got it right. "Jews demand signs," said Paul (1 Corinthians 1:22), and these signs were apparently becoming scarce by A.D. 65. Whereas the Christian faith was born in an atmosphere of "signs, wonders and various miracles, and . . . gifts of the Holy Spirit" (Hebrews 2:4), it seems there was a diminishing of these phenomena some thirty years later.

The supernatural manifestations of the Holy Spirit on the Day of Pentecost led to three thousand conversions of Jews, the fear of God on every soul and an unusual sense of the unity of the Holy Spirit (Acts 2). But many of these converts were from outside Jerusalem, having come there for the annual feast of Pentecost. This left a core of converted Jews in Jerusalem. However, the miracle of the handicapped man being suddenly healed led to thousands more conversions (Acts 3, 4:4). For a while it must have seemed that the Christian faith would take off among the Jews and become the wave of the future. That did not happen. The edict of the Sanhedrin had a wide and intimidating influence. Stephen, the first deacon of the Church—who also addressed the Sanhedrin with extraordinary power—was nonetheless rejected and became the first martyr to be welcomed home (Acts 7:55–60). Because persecution was now on the increase, all believers except the apostles fled Jerusalem (Acts 8:1). The Sanhedrin won the day; the wave of the future pointed to Gentiles, not Jews, coming to Christ.

The epistle to the Hebrews addresses Christian Jews, before A.D. 70, who were very discouraged for several reasons. First, as long as there were signs and wonders, the Jews who accepted Jesus Christ could appear vindicated and feel rewarded for their faith. But as signs happened less and less, the stigma increased more and more. Second, the number of Jews meeting for worship, study and fellowship was not rising. Small numbers, especially when they are decreasing more and more, are very discouraging. The writer of Hebrews cautions them not to forsake assembling together "as some are in the habit of doing" (Hebrews 10:25). Low numbers was not a good testimony to the world—and dampened the spirits of believers, especially when unbelieving Jews got word of their lack of success.

✝ EXTERNAL VINDICATION

All the above can be summed up as follows: These Hebrew Christians were discouraged because of the withholding of vindication, that is, external vindication. God was also hiding His face from them for a while for some reason. God does this sort of thing (Isaiah 45:15; Psalm 13:1), leaving us with a feeling of being deserted. It was accompanied by the absence of visible evidence that God was blessing and owning them. They had no external proof—miracles, success, increasing numbers of Jews being converted—of the validity of their decision to affirm Jesus of Nazareth as having been raised from the dead. If only God would step in and do something like destroy the Temple—which Jesus promised would happen—then they could point to their fellow Jews and say, "See there—Jesus told us it would be destroyed"! But it was A.D. 60–65 and the Temple was still standing and thriving. There was no hint that God had written "Ichabod" (the glory has departed) over the Temple. As for the curtain in the Temple, which had been torn in two from top to bottom when Jesus died on the cross (Matthew 27:51), either someone had sewed it back up or they had got a new curtain. People continued to go to the Temple to worship and that edifice stood as stately and undisturbed as ever. The Temple was actually destroyed not that long afterward, in A.D. 70, but it was alive and well when the book of Hebrews was written.

One of the most important reasons behind the writing of the epistle to the Hebrews was that Jews needed to learn that signs and wonders are not everything. They needed doctrine. They needed to know how the Law had been fulfilled by Jesus' work on the cross. They needed to know that Jesus fulfilled David's word about the priesthood being "after the order of Melchizedek" (Psalm 110:4; Hebrews 7:11–17). They needed to see the proper place of the Tabernacle in God's scheme of things. They needed to know that they were all invited to be in the succession of the great men and women of faith (Hebrews 12:1). As Dr. Martyn Lloyd-Jones used to say, "A discouraged church doesn't need encouragement, it needs doctrine." They needed to learn the doctrine of God's chastening, or disciplining (Hebrews 12:5–11).

A lack of vindication, painful though it is, can be the best thing that happens to us. Losing that 1955 Chevrolet did me no harm. I needed to be dependent on God alone—not my dad, my godly grandmother, Billy Ball or other friends. That was over fifty years ago. We now live near Nashville, Tennessee, and go by the same Chevrolet dealer (where that car came from) all the time—a reminder of those days. I had no future in any church after I left Trevecca in 1956. I was forced to stay in secular work to pay my bills.

The writer of Hebrews did not promise these Hebrew Christians vindication that would cause their fellow Jews to applaud them but guaranteed only a very wonderful relationship with

God. He promised them they could fulfill the Sabbath rest internally, come into full assurance of faith and hope, experience God swearing an oath to them like He had done to Abraham and even succeed those famous people of faith—doing in their day what the people described in Hebrews 11 did in theirs. He told them not to give up: "God is not unjust; he will not forget your work and the love you have shown him" (Hebrews 6:10). Do not "throw away your confidence"; after all, "He who is coming will come and will not delay" (Hebrews 10:35, 37)—a reference not so much to the Second Coming of Jesus as it was to inheriting this extraordinary relationship with God.

It was internal vindication that was on offer. External vindication is when you are openly cleared—others applaud you. Internal vindication is when God says "well done"; it is experiencing the honor that comes only from Him (John 5:44). It may or may not have been what they had been hoping for, but it is what the writer set before their eyes.

† INTERNAL VINDICATION

Jesus' vindication was internal. This is what Paul meant by Jesus' being "vindicated by the Spirit" (1 Timothy 3:16, also ESV). It is the internal witness of the Spirit. With Jesus it was an internal witness without limit (John 3:34). It was the source of His joy and pleasure. He did not look to the applause of people. He did not turn to one of His disciples after finishing the Sermon on the Mount to ask, "How do you think I did?" Jesus lived for one thing: pleasing His Father (John 8:29). He did nothing by Himself but kept His eyes on the Father (John 5:19)—living for and by His approval. His vindication was internal—being infallibly and marvelously assured in His spirit that He had gotten it right.

His internal vindication is what kept Him going in Gethsemane, before Herod, before Pilate and on the cross. The only time it was withheld was when the Father turned His back on Him and Jesus cried out, "My God, my God, why have you forsaken me?" (Matthew 27:46). Even after Jesus was raised from the dead He refused to seek external vindication. He did not show up on Easter morning on Herod's or Pilate's doorstep and say, "Surprise!" He only appeared to Mary Magdalene, then the Eleven and eventually five hundred (1 Corinthians 15:6). But these were already believers. Jesus' vindication became external only when He returned to heaven—when the angels welcomed Him, the sainted dead (I like to think) witnessed His return and the Father said, "Sit at my right hand."

Our vindication so far is internal; that is, we have no external proof that Jesus is the God-man who was raised from the dead and is now seated in glory at the Father's right hand. We confess Him as Lord, yes. But it is by faith (Hebrews 11:1). We cannot point to any sign that infallibly vindicates us before people. Therefore our vindication, like that of Jesus, is internal.

That will change. One day "every knee" shall bow and "every tongue" shall confess that Jesus Christ is Lord. That is when Jesus—and we—will be externally vindicated. But now we live by faith.

As for the hiding of God's face from these Hebrew Christians, that is the essential ingredient in being chastened, or disciplined. The Greek word means *enforced learning*. God teaches us what we need to learn, not what we would like others to see about us. I remember crying out one August day in 1956—without a car, without the approval of my family and with no future that I could see, "Why? Why Lord? You told me You were going to use me." In that moment I felt an impulse to turn to Hebrews 12:6, so I did. There it was, my introduction to a teaching I had not considered: "Whom the Lord loveth he chasteneth, and scourgeth every son whom he receiveth" (KJV). That verse would not be out of my mind from that day on.

I learned countless lessons over the years, while I waited for my ministry to finally arrive. I learned not only how to handle money but how to deal with people. I sometimes think all ministers should have to live in the real world for a while before they enter ministry. One of the chief and most valuable lessons I learned, however, was the principle of vindication—it is what *God* does. By Himself. Without our lifting a finger. It is also what God does best. He does not like it one bit when we try to help Him. Like justification by faith, works do not help; He wants all the glory. So, too, with vindication; our efforts do not help, they only hinder. God wants all the glory. It means waiting. Sometimes it means waiting for a long while.

I believe God wanted to teach me internal vindication before I could handle external vindication. Keep in mind that Jesus' internal vindication was having total awareness of His Father's approval because He had the Holy Spirit without any limit (John 3:34). You and I have only a limit, or measure, of the Spirit (Romans 12:3). We need, nonetheless, to make every effort to obtain the praise and honor that comes from God alone (John 5:44). It is therefore possible for you and me to have internal vindication but still long for external vindication. But we should learn to be content with internal vindication. Doing so is "great gain" (1 Timothy 6:6). In my case, I also believe that God wanted me to learn a lot of things at the purely human level, as well as getting to know His Word—and some good, sound theology—before I could be trusted with the approval of my dad.

But that day came—22 years later, in 1978, on a train from Edinburgh to London. About an hour before we arrived at King's Cross Station, Dad looked at me and said, "Son, I'm proud of you. I am proud to be your father. You were right, I was wrong. Will you forgive me?" The stigma of lack of vindication—at least where my dad was concerned—was now gone. It was a pretty wonderful feeling, I can tell you. But had that come 22 years earlier I would not have learned the lessons I needed desperately to grasp.

The Hebrew Christians were not seeking internal vindication; they wanted their fellow Jews to approve of them. That never came, sadly. But the one thing they were promised was an intimate relationship with the Holy Spirit. They possibly could not appreciate this when it was first offered. But if they waited and experienced it, they would learn that it does not get better than that.

11

THE STIGMA
OF SUSPICION

Is this not Jesus, the son of Joseph, whose father and mother we know?

— John 6:42

But Mary treasured up all these things and pondered them in her heart.

— Luke 2:19

Suspicion means doubt over someone's honesty. It is when you question their integrity, genuineness or reliability. It is a painful thing to endure when you know in your heart of hearts that people generally feel suspicious about you.

Joseph and Mary, Jesus' parents, endured the pain of poisonous suspicion all their lives. It is what the people of Galilee generally suspected—or wanted to believe—all along about Jesus; namely, that He was the illegitimate child of Joseph and Mary. Their suspicions were only vocalized, however, when Jesus began to displease the crowds that had gathered after His feeding of the five thousand with five loaves and two fish. As long as He was changing water into wine, healing people of their illnesses and feeding thousands with loaves and fish the people were more than willing to dismiss such unthinkable and despicable rumors—and to gladly accept Him. They were even determined to make Him king (John 6:15)! But once Jesus began to teach things that offended them—as His sermon of "hard sayings" unfolded in John 6—all those suspicions surfaced with a vengeance and the people blurted out what they all now preferred after all to believe about His background. That is precisely what lay behind the question, "Is this not Jesus, the son of Joseph, whose father and mother we know?" (John 6:42). The people must have felt that knowing where Jesus came from now exempted them from having to believe His teaching.

† KEEPING A SECRET

Imagine living with a stigma like this. Joseph and Mary knew the truth. But rather than try to vindicate themselves—as if anybody would believe their story—they lived with a secret.

The psalmist said that the "secret of the LORD is with them that fear him" (Psalm 25:14, KJV; "The LORD confides in those who fear him," NIV). This is an amazing word. Can there be a greater honor than to have the Lord God of heaven and earth confide in you? To share a secret with you? He "confides" in those who fear Him—that is, He respects those so much because He knows they will not repeat what He said to them.

Can you keep a secret? Most people cannot. They will say they can when, in fact, they have to tell *somebody* when something good has happened to them or when they have heard something about someone else. It is a remarkable person who can absolutely *not tell anybody* what they know—whom they met or what flattering thing was bestowed on them. This is especially true with divine revelation. I truly believe that God would share more things with us if we could keep quiet about it—telling *nobody anything* about what we have received from Him. It is sometimes said that Her Majesty the Queen is the loneliest person in the world. Who can she confide in? Who would hear her say something in private and not tell it? She therefore keeps countless feelings and opinions to herself.

A well-known Englishman, famous for his cynicism, surprised people when he actually agreed to accept a knighthood from the queen. When asked why he accepted it, he replied, "Nobody should turn down a knighthood unless they can keep quiet about it. I knew I couldn't, so I accepted it." Honest man!

Joseph and Mary had to live with a secret and stigma *all their lives*. They would be secretly accused of conceiving a baby—Jesus of Nazareth—out of wedlock. Not a stigma today, but it certainly was then.

† THE VIRGIN BIRTH OF JESUS

It all began in Nazareth. The angel Gabriel appeared to Mary, a virgin living in Nazareth, and said, "Greetings, you who are highly favored! The Lord is with you." This troubled her. But the angel put her mind at rest: "Do not be afraid, Mary; you have found favor with God." Then came the promise that she would "conceive and give birth to a son, and you are to call him Jesus. He will be great and will be called the Son of the Most High." But Mary could only think of one thing: "How will this be . . . since I am a virgin?" The angel answered that the Holy Spirit would come upon her and the power of the Most High God would overshadow her. She would give birth to the "Son of God" (Luke 1:28–35). After all, concluded Gabriel, "Nothing is impossible with God."

At this stage Mary could have backed out of this. She might have said, "Let me think about it," "I don't believe you" or "This is too much stuff to take on board at this point in my life." I have wondered if perhaps when we go to heaven ourselves, we will get to watch a kind of DVD of what was happening in heaven at that point. The Second Person of the Godhead, known only as the Word—logos—was waiting for the moment when He would leave His heavenly place with God—for He was God—and take on human flesh. Were the angels watching? One thing is certain: He would remain in heaven with God until Mary gave a positive response. She wasted no time. "I am the Lord's servant," she replied. "May your word to me be fulfilled" (Luke 1:38). At that very moment the Eternal Logos left heaven for earth and entered the womb of Mary to become human flesh and be born Son of

God—never to be the same again. He said in heaven, envisaging His future existence, "a body you prepared for me" (Hebrews 10:5). When the Word entered the Virgin Mary, the embryo was already a body, a body that would grow and develop and be born into a world that He made, but which would reject Him.

By the way, the virgin birth—which is a stigma for us, because the world scoffs at the idea, let alone the sad fact that a lot of professing Christians do not believe it anymore—is nonetheless an apt tool to use as a testimony to Muslims. All Muslims believe in the virgin birth of Jesus. One of Yasser Arafat's first comments to me was, "Did you know that the only woman mentioned in the Koran is the Virgin Mary?" I replied, "Then you are saying that the Koran affirms Jesus as the Son of God—who had no earthly father?" He changed the subject, for it is something that can be rightly used when witnessing to a Muslim.

Mary had a dilemma. How should she tell Joseph? Would he believe her? Imagine the work cut out for Mary—telling Joseph she was pregnant. Apparently he initially told her that he honestly did not know what to believe! Matthew's account takes up the story. The angel (presumably Gabriel again) said to him in a dream,

> Joseph son of David, do not be afraid to take Mary home as your wife, because what is conceived in her is from the Holy Spirit. She will give birth to a son, and you are to give him the name Jesus, because he will save his people from their sins.
>
> — *Matthew 1:20–21*

When he woke up, the man who would become the unsung hero of Christmas "did what the angel of the Lord had commanded him and took Mary home as his wife" (Matthew 1:24). It took courage for Mary to say, "Yes Lord" to the angel, but perhaps even more courage for Joseph to agree to all this. He might have conveniently cancelled their engagement. He was a "righteous man," meaning not only that he had been sexually pure with Mary, but that he did not want to embarrass Mary by revealing that she was pregnant (Matthew 1:19). He struggled with her story when he learned that she was pregnant. But having once agreed to stay with her, it meant that people would never, never, never believe their story—even if he told it around. So all he could do was to keep quiet about it—and let people think the worst. They no doubt did.

One of the more interesting things regarding this scenario is that the twelve disciples may also have been privy to these rumors. If so, it made no difference to them (as far as we know). When Jesus brought His "hard sayings" sermon to a close, the crowd of thousands deserted Him right, left and center. "From this time many of his disciples [other followers, not the Twelve] turned back and no longer followed him." "You do not want to leave too, do you?" Jesus asked the Twelve. Simon Peter answered Him, "Lord, to whom shall we go? You have the words of eternal life. We have come to believe and know that you are the Holy One of God" (John 6:66–69).

It is my view that Mary kept the details of Jesus' birth between herself and Joseph for many years. I cannot prove it, but I take the view (certainly not original with me) that the truth of the virgin birth was disclosed to a few, long after Jesus' death, resurrection and ascension. "Mary treasured up all these things and pondered them in her heart" (Luke 2:19). She later lived in Ephesus, near John, who had been commanded by Jesus to look after her (John 19:27). It may have been there that she told Luke the story—about Gabriel, the journey to Bethlehem, the innkeeper, the birth, the shepherds, the circumcision, Simeon, Anna and what happened when Jesus accompanied Joseph and her to Jerusalem at the age of twelve (Luke 2).

Sometimes God puts a stigma on us that we could not shake off even if we tried. It is not unlike Paul's "thorn in the flesh"; he prayed three times that it might depart but only got the answer, "My grace is sufficient for you, for my power is made perfect in weakness" (2 Corinthians 12:9). You could say that the stigma on Joseph and Mary was much like that. They were helpless to make it go away. They were hemmed in. For who would have believed them had they told what actually happened?

If I am correct in my opinion, that even the Twelve did not know until years later the truth about the virgin birth of Jesus that you and I know, it is somewhat remarkable—knowing the rumors—that this did not hinder their putting their faith in Jesus. It means they, too, accepted and lived with a stigma of knowing what was out there in the public arena—and they stayed loyal to Jesus.

You and I have the privilege of affirming God for being just and holy when we still do not have all the information we would like—we may wonder why He lets things happen that we do not understand. God could clear His Name—and ours—at any moment if He chose to, but we must wait for His sovereign timing. And, after all, what if vindication—His and ours—is postponed until the Last Day when every knee shall bow and every tongue confess that Jesus Christ is Lord (Philippians 2:9–11)? One day, God will reveal facts that might have vindicated Him long ago. For the most stigmatized person in the universe is God the Father.

I remember being in the middle of a terrific struggle, feeling betrayed and knowing that what was being said about me was not true, but unable to set the record straight. My eyes fell on these words:

> All this is evidence that God's judgment is right, and as a result you will be counted worthy of the kingdom of God, for which you are suffering. God is just: He will pay

back trouble to those who trouble you and give relief to you who are troubled, and to us as well.

— *2 Thessalonians 1:5–7*

I thought, *Oh good. Nice. Wonderful. Thank you, Lord*. Until I noticed Paul wasn't finished, for he continued: "This will happen when the Lord Jesus is revealed from heaven in blazing fire with his powerful angels." I thought, *Oh no. Do I have to wait that long?*

The truth is, sooner or later all of us will be invited to join the ranks of those who suffered before us. We are called to do in our day what they did in theirs. And the stigma may be just as painful as theirs.

What a privilege, then, to mirror the stigma of Joseph and Mary, the stigma of Jesus and the stigma of God. Joseph and Mary did not defend themselves; God does not defend Himself; you and I must not be too anxious to defend ourselves—whether we are falsely accused or merely under suspicion.

† CONTROLLING THE TONGUE

A heart-searching proverb is this: "Sin is not ended by multiplying words, but the prudent hold their tongues" (Proverbs 10:19). Moreover, "The prudent keep their knowledge to themselves" (Proverbs 12:23). It takes a lot of self-discipline to keep quiet when you are, as it were, sitting on knowledge that would clear things up.

Take the principle of total forgiveness, for example. The severest temptation of all when we have been maligned is to tell somebody—the more, the better. It is our way of punishing the person who has hurt us and making ourselves feel better. But the first principle of total forgiveness is that we tell nobody what "they" did to us. As Joseph, the favorite son of Jacob, would not let anybody know what his brothers had so wickedly done to him (Genesis 45), so you and I must never—ever—tell "what they did." We may well be sitting on knowledge that would clear things up—and make us look good. But to do so would be to violate a very important principle—namely, that vengeance belongs to God (Romans 12:19). This means we must stay absolutely quiet about the very thing that would clear our names.

That is what Joseph and Mary had to do for many, many years. All the suspicions of her being pregnant prior to their marriage would be part of the stigma God imposed on them from the start. Mary's word—"May it be to me as you have said"—was to accept the stigma. Joseph's obedience—doing "what the angel of the Lord had commanded him"—was to accept the stigma. For the whole of their lives Joseph would be the man who got Mary pregnant before they got married.

Controlling the tongue when you could so easily clear things up is a very hard thing to do. But it is the way we demonstrate before God that we accept the stigma He has chosen for us. I am fond of the old spiritual:

> Nobody knows de trouble I've seen
> Nobody knows but Jesus
> Nobody knows de trouble I've seen
> Glory Hallelujah!
>
> — *Anon.*

Like so many of the spirituals that came out of America's Deep South in the awful times of slavery, this spiritual is profound. Notice that *only Jesus knows*—nobody else; what is more, "Glory Hallelujah!" Think about that—Glory Hallelujah! when only God knows. When others know about your troubles, it means you have the support of people around you—which we all need from time to time. But when Jesus is the *only* one to know, He is

153

especially honored. It means He is the only one "in the know" and that you did not tell Him plus a thousand others to feel better or get joy; you got satisfaction from knowing He alone knows what you have been through. It singularly honors Him and God will further honor you, too! This is a way we get the unique praise that comes only from Him because we kept things from everyone else (John 5:44).

Bearing the stigma always implies the challenge of tongue control. This is possibly the hardest thing to learn. "We all stumble in many ways. Anyone who is never at fault in what they say is perfect, able to keep their whole body in check" (James 3:2). And yet we are to be stirred to make every effort. "Do you see someone who speaks in haste? There is more hope for a fool than for them" (Proverbs 29:20). This means I have been a fool more times than I care to think about.

We need therefore to keep quiet about (1) things God has been pleased to reveal to us and (2) saying what might clear our names when God says that we must let Him do it, His way.

Can anything be more hurtful for a young woman than to live in her own community and to be under the suspicion that she conceived Jesus before she and Joseph were properly married? She must have yearned to tell the truth. She did in fact tell her cousin Elizabeth (Luke 1:39–55), but that was not with the intention of clearing her name. She wanted to share the thrilling news and she was led by the Spirit to reveal this.

Sometimes we are permitted to tell what we know, *not* because we want to make ourselves look good but to encourage those around us who cannot figure out what is going on. In other words, we want *them* to feel better. But there are times we cannot do that either. I have often thought that Jesus would love to have sent word—even from the cross—to Mary Magdalene, who was bewildered and sobbing her heart out over what was happening: "Don't worry, Mary, what I am doing is why I came into this world. I am dying for the sins of the world. What is taking place is not an accident or tragedy—however unjust it may be; I am atoning for sin. So don't worry." But no. Part of His suffering was to see her suffer.

And in the same way, part of the stigma—and the pain of it—which we must bear is not being able to make our friends feel better about us. The stigma even includes being misunderstood by those who love us, as well as by those who hate us.

† POSTHUMOUS VINDICATION

One final question: What if you were told that vindication will come to you after you are in heaven? What if there is *no vindication* while you are alive, but only after you die? Could you live with that?

The vindication of Joseph and Mary was posthumous. Mary was indeed highly favored—truly blessed among women. But not in her lifetime. Mary exulted, "From now on all generations will call me blessed" (Luke 1:48). Joseph is honored today by all of us. But not in his lifetime either.

Forgive me if this seems a bit unfair, but if you had a choice between being vindicated in your lifetime and being honored after your death—and way beyond—which would you choose? You do not have to answer that question. But one thing you and I must be willing to do is to keep quiet when it comes to clearing our names here on earth. Vindication is God's domain. And whether He chooses to vindicate us now or later will not matter when we are in heaven. We will be thrilled in heaven whichever way God chose to do it here below. Let us be thrilled now—whichever it is.

12

The Stigma of the Holy Spirit

Some, however, made fun of them and said, "They have had too much wine."

— *Acts 2:13*

We are witnesses of these things, and so is the Holy Spirit, whom God has given to those who obey him.

— *Acts 5:32*

The stigma that the Virgin Mary bore was the result of the Holy Spirit. All that followed after her expression of willingness to the angel Gabriel came from the Holy Spirit. She had been told, "The Holy Spirit will come on you, and the power of the Most High will overshadow you" (Luke 1:35). The stigma that Mary and Joseph would bear after that was the result of the Holy Spirit's work. It is not superficially obvious, but we could say that the stigma they bore was that of the Holy Spirit, who set these events in motion.

The truth is that all three persons of the Trinity have their own stigma. The stigma of God is that He is the most maligned person in the universe. He refuses to clear His Name in advance of the Final Judgment. So once we submit to His will we bear His stigma. What a privilege! Second, there is the stigma of the Son of God—Jesus Christ. We have seen the stigma of the Gospel. He said, "If the world hates you, keep in mind that it hated me first" (John 15:18). "Do not be surprised, my brothers and sisters, if the world hates you" (1 John 3:13). That is the stigma of Jesus. But in this chapter we examine the stigma of the Holy Spirit—the Third Person of the Godhead. When you remember that we defined stigma as being an embarrassment that you cannot explain away, you will see in this chapter that possibly the most embarrassing stigma of all is that of the Holy Spirit.

The obvious public stigma of the Spirit surfaced on the Day of Pentecost, when people mocked the 120 disciples who had been filled with the Spirit, accusing them of being drunk (Acts 2:13). But behind that stigma was the bold claim that the Holy

Spirit had told them where Jesus was! Having claimed that Jesus was raised from the dead, the most natural question was, "Then where is He?" Peter claimed that Jesus had been "exalted to the right hand of God," fulfilling the word of David, "The Lord said to my Lord: 'Sit at my right hand until I make your enemies a footstool for your feet'" (Acts 2:34–35). The initial stigma of the Holy Spirit in the early Church, then, was two-fold: (1) how foolish the disciples appeared because of their behavior and (2) how foolish they seemed because of their impossible-to-prove claim that Jesus was now at God's right hand! That would be seen as a convenient cop-out, since nobody could disprove this kind of claim. But the disciples could not prove it either. Furthermore, the witness of the Holy Spirit was *so real* to them that they could truthfully say that there was a two-fold witness to Jesus' resurrection: (1) the disciples had literally seen Him in flesh with their own eyes after He was raised from the dead, and (2) the Holy Spirit Himself *witnessed to them*—that is, *told them*—where Jesus was! They looked foolish to the Jews making such a claim; they looked stupid because of their behavior and foolish because of their assertion that Jesus was in heaven at God's right hand.

† LOOKING FOOLISH

We begin with the way the 120—at least some of them—appeared to onlookers on the Day of Pentecost. There were supernatural phenomena that accompanied the coming of the Spirit. The Day of Pentecost—fifty days after Passover—was also the commemoration of the giving of the Law at Sinai. Thousands of Jews were present, from about twenty countries, for this annual feast. God decided to surprise everybody that year! While thousands were gathered for this feast, 120 were gathered in an

Upper Room in Jerusalem, praying and waiting for the Spirit which Jesus had promised (Luke 24:49; Acts 1:4, 8).

"Suddenly a sound like the blowing of a violent wind came from heaven and filled the whole house where they were sitting." Luke says that not only those in the Upper Room, but those present outside for the Day of Pentecost "heard this sound," possibly meaning the violent wind but certainly also their noisy speaking in other languages inside, as we will see below. One hundred and twenty people were ecstatic, thrilled, joyful, not being self-conscious but loudly manifesting the Spirit by speaking in other languages. In other words, you did not need to be in the Upper Room to hear what was going on. You could hear their raised voices proclaiming the "wonders of God" a distance away. But you needed to be inside to see what the 120 witnessed. They looked at each other and saw "what seemed to be tongues of fire that separated and came to rest on each of them." What a moment that must have been. All of them—not just some—were filled with the Holy Spirit and "began to speak in other tongues as the Spirit enabled them" (Acts 2:2–4).

The sound that everybody heard drew a crowd of people, who flocked near the Upper Room in bewilderment. What startled the people was that "each one heard them speaking in his own language." They asked, "Aren't all these who are speaking Galileans? Then how is it that each of us hears them in our native language?" (Acts 2:5–8). The miracle was both in the speaking in other languages but also in the hearing of them. Though these Galileans spoke in their native Hebrew or Aramaic, you heard it in Arabic if you were from Arabia, probably Latin if you were from Rome, Greek if you were from Crete. "We hear them declaring the wonders of God in our own tongues!" (Acts 2:11).

There were two reactions from those outside. First, those who were "amazed and perplexed," who soberly and in awe asked one another, "What does this mean?" Second, there were

THE STIGMA OF THE HOLY SPIRIT

the mockers who made fun of them and said, "They have had too much wine" (Acts 2:12–13). I doubt that the miracle of the language phenomena made them poke fun. It scared them. Hearing their own languages—though spoken by the Galileans—is what, in my opinion, "amazed and perplexed" the people. So, the language phenomena is not what caused people to make fun of them. The opposite is true: The phenomena regarding the languages is what made them stand in awe and amazement. I have come to the view that what made them mock is something rather different. My suspicion is that many of those 120 not only spoke in other languages but were filled with so much joy that they could not sit or stand but fell down and possibly rolled on the floor—laughing their heads off. Seeing people like this myself has helped me come to this point of view. I suspect that when we get to heaven we will learn it was this kind of strange behavior of those followers of Jesus on the Day of Pentecost—not the speaking or hearing of languages—that lay behind the accusation of their being drunk. When Paul later said one should not be drunk with wine but "filled with the Spirit" (Ephesians 5:18), it was partly because being filled with the Spirit can sometimes cause a person to appear that they are drunk.

I was speaking at a conference in a hotel where some of the people were so enjoying the teaching, worship and time of ministry that they behaved as if they were drunk. I will never forget going up in the elevator in the same hotel where the conference was held only to find people in the elevator who were unable to stand but were sitting on the floor of the elevator, laughing their heads off. It was impossible to know whether these people had come out of the bar of the hotel or from the conference. I could not tell the difference. Although this has not happened to me, I have seen others manifest like this. I have even seen this happen to some after I myself have prayed for them! Why it has not happened to me, I do not know. But I am willing for it to happen.

Yes, the Holy Spirit has His own stigma. It may be because of an overt manifestation as I have just described, and which may seem off-putting, even disgusting, to some—especially sophisticated people. It may be the stigma that one bears because of the way the Holy Spirit comes on them and leads them, as in the case of Joseph and Mary. It may be like that of the disciples, who were regarded as unworthy to be taken seriously because of their claim that Jesus was raised from the dead. Their critics noted that those such as Peter and John were uneducated and "ordinary men" who were known to have been with Jesus (Acts 4:13).

† THE WITNESS OF THE SPIRIT

A witness is one who sees an event and reports what happened. It is a person who can give a firsthand account of what was seen, heard or experienced. The apostles had seen Jesus in the flesh after He was raised from the dead. They saw both His being "killed by hanging him on a cross" and also saw Him in His risen body. "We are witnesses of these things" refers to their being eyewitnesses of Jesus' death and resurrection. But they added, "And so is the Holy Spirit" (Acts 5:30–32). So we are talking about two witnesses: physical and spiritual. One was at the natural level, the other being supernatural.

The witness of the Holy Spirit—as experienced by the apostles—made the fact of the bodily resurrection of Jesus *as real as seeing Him* with their own eyes. They could not say one witness made Jesus' resurrection more real than the other, whether it was their being eyewitnesses—seeing Jesus alive after His death—or having the Holy Spirit make this real. The latter is what Dr. Martyn Lloyd-Jones used to call the "immediate and direct witness" of the Holy Spirit. Hence the apostles' statement, "We are witnesses of these things, *and so is the Holy Spirit*" (Acts 5:32, emphasis mine). The Third Person of the Trinity made Jesus' resurrection as real to them as if it were right there before their very eyes. Not that the members of the Sanhedrin would believe them when they said, "So is the Holy Spirit," but Peter and John knew what they were talking about.

They added one caveat: "Whom God has given to those who obey him" (Acts 5:32). The Holy Spirit does not witness to everybody, say Peter and the apostles, but only to those who obey God. Those who waited in the Upper Room for ten days (the time between Jesus' ascension and the Day of Pentecost) were there in obedience. Jesus told them to "wait," so they did. Their staying in Jerusalem until the Spirit fell on them was worth waiting for.

The Holy Spirit is given to those who receive the Gospel. All who receive the Gospel—who know their sins are forgiven through the sacrifice of Jesus Christ—are given the Holy Spirit. "And if anyone does not have the Spirit of Christ, they do not belong to Christ" (Romans 8:9). It is the Holy Spirit who gives life, said Jesus in His sermon of the "hard sayings" (John 6:63). This life is called regeneration, or being born again (John 3:3). It is usually an unconscious work of the Spirit. There may be exceptions. There are those who receive a conscious witness of the Spirit at conversion, like Cornelius (Acts 10). But more often than not regeneration is an unconscious work of the Spirit. There are those who insist they can tell you the "day and the hour" when they were converted, granted. But the Spirit of God was at work in them *before* that moment, although they may not have been aware of it. Some tell you they can tell you the "day and the hour" when they knew they were saved, granted. But this probably refers to *assurance* of salvation, not salvation itself. As for those who fear they are not saved because they cannot point to the "day and the hour," they should take comfort from Augustus Toplady's (author of "Rock of Ages") comment: "You may know the sun is up although you were not awake the moment it arose."

What happened, then, on the Day of Pentecost? Were the 120 regenerated on that day? I answer: They were regenerated before then. But when the Spirit fell on them it was the "highest level of assurance," to quote Dr. Lloyd-Jones again. Whether you call it baptism, being filled or sealed with the Spirit, the 120 experienced an immediate and direct witness of the Spirit that gave them an infallible assurance of salvation, an unashamed boldness and unspeakable joy. They were without any fear whatsoever. The person of Jesus was as real to them as if He had showed up before their very eyes.

Are all who are converted given this measure of assurance? Probably not. This does not mean they do not have the Holy Spirit, because if you do not have the Holy Spirit you do not belong to Christ, as we saw above (Romans 8:9). But there are *degrees* of assurance. This does not mean some are more "saved" than others, because if you are saved, you are *saved*. But not all have the same measure of the Spirit and not all have the same level of assurance of salvation.

Driving my Chevrolet back to Trevecca, where I was a student, on October 31, 1955, I had what I often call a "Damascus Road" experience. Perhaps I should not call it that because I was already converted, whereas Paul was actually converted when he was confronted by Jesus on his way to Damascus (Acts 9:1–9). I call it that because it was then that the person of Jesus Christ became as real to me as if He were sitting in the car with me. As I drove, there was Jesus interceding for me. He seemed to be putting His authority with the Father on the line. I never felt so loved in all my life! I heard Jesus say to the Father (referring to me), "He wants it." I heard the Father reply, "He can have it." In that moment I felt my heart warmed. I felt a peace that was beyond anything I had ever experienced. The person of

Jesus was so real to me. All this happened as I drove. For days afterward He was more real to me than anybody around me. I was given a full assurance of my salvation, as I related a little bit earlier in this book.

My encounter with the risen, ascended and interceding Christ on that day is precisely why I know what Peter and John meant when they said, "And so is the Holy Spirit." I am a witness to the fact that the Spirit can make Jesus as real as if He were physically present. I did not become "more saved" that day; I was already saved forever. But from that day on I never again— ever—doubted my salvation.

The stigma of the Spirit's witness was that it offended many around me that I could make the claim that I knew without any doubt whatsoever that I would go to heaven when I die. The further offense was that it led me to certain teachings that went against my old denomination's interpretation of the Bible. This is why my father and grandmother were so upset with me at the time.

† SPEAKING IN TONGUES

Some readers will want to know, "Did you speak in tongues that day?" The answer is no, I did not. There are those who will say this means I was not baptized with the Holy Spirit. The terminology is not so important to me. Call it what you will, I only knew I was infallibly sealed and assured of my salvation—and that I was given full assurance of understanding of certain doctrines (Colossians 2:2).

However, several months later—also driving my car, this time coming from Kentucky and just as we were approaching the Tennessee border—I unexpectedly felt a stirring in my heart. It would be more honest if I said the stirring was in my stomach because that is where the feeling was. Like a well that wanted to spring up. It was as if the well would not spring up unless I spoke what came to me, and out of my mouth—to my amazement—came unintelligible sounds. It lasted only seconds. But I knew, like it or not—although Nazarenes were dead set against this sort of thing—that I had spoken in tongues. I told no one for years and years and years. I did tell this to Dr. Lloyd-Jones after I became the minister at Westminster Chapel in 1977, wondering what he would think. He replied, "I always said I would believe a person spoke in tongues if it happened to them only once." That was his answer.

However, in 1993—when I was at the height of one of the greatest crises of my life—I cried out to God. Speaking in tongues was revived that day and I have been doing it ever since.

I have had a number of doors closed to me because of what I have related above and because I preach to a lot of different people, crossing denominational and theological lines. In some places, speaking in tongues gives great offense. You can be guilty of adultery and be forgiven; you can be a Mason and be accepted; but if you ever speak in tongues you will never be forgiven or accepted—at least in this world.

I am not ashamed of the Gospel. I am not ashamed of the Holy Spirit or His manifestations and I am not ashamed of speaking in tongues. It was never my idea in the first place! But it is—for me—part of the whole stigma of following the Lord in obedience, wherever it may lead.

13

Manifestations of the Holy Spirit

When the crowds heard Philip and saw the signs he performed, they all paid close attention to what he said. For with shrieks, impure spirits came out of many, and many who were paralyzed or lame were healed. So there was great joy in that city.

— Acts 8:6–8

God chose the foolish things of the world to shame the wise . . . the weak things of the world to shame the strong . . . the lowly things of this world and the despised things . . . so that no one may boast before him.

— 1 Corinthians 1:27–29

The Trinity of most Evangelicals today is God the Father, God the Son and God the Holy Bible.

— Jack Taylor

The word *manifestation* means demonstration, sign, epiphany, revelation, display or expression. The paramount manifestation—or demonstration—of the Holy Spirit was on the Day of Pentecost, with the rushing of the mighty wind, the tongues of fire and the speaking in other languages—and their simultaneous translation to those who heard the 120 speaking. There is a sense, however, in which the whole book of Acts is essentially a disclosure of one manifestation of the Spirit after another. Some scholars have suggested that the title of Acts could be Acts of the Holy Spirit instead of the traditional Acts of the Apostles. The list, if you tried to compile it, would be a long one.

† EXAMPLES OF MANIFESTATIONS IN ACTS

For example, *preaching* heads the list if you begin to see how the Holy Spirit moved after the Spirit fell on the 120. The first thing Peter did was to explain to everyone what was happening and then to use the platform to preach the Gospel. The next manifestation of the Spirit would be the *conviction* of the Spirit upon the hearers when they were "cut to the heart" and said to Peter and the other apostles, "Brothers, what shall we do?" (Acts 2:37). Behind this conviction was the work of the Spirit in converting three thousand people, who were immediately baptized. The Spirit manifested Himself after that in the people devoting themselves to teaching, fellowship, observance of the Lord's Supper and prayer (Acts 2:42). At the bottom of all that was going on was the fear of God—"everyone was filled with awe"—a supernatural manifestation of the Holy Spirit. Then comes "wonders and signs" that were done by the apostles (Acts 2:43). Along with this came an extraordinary unity of the Spirit when all the believers "had everything in common," "selling their property and possessions" and giving to "anyone who had need" (Acts 2:44–45).

There was such a high level of the Spirit upon the Church in those days that I doubt there was any sense of stigma—that is, shame or embarrassment—in the conscious thinking of those who experienced this. The truth is, when the Spirit comes in great power the sense of embarrassment is a non-issue. It is when the Holy Spirit seems to lift, or diminish, that embarrassment creeps in. As long as the Holy Spirit is on and in a person in great power that person loses a sense of self-consciousness, shame or embarrassment. When Peter and John rejoiced over the privilege of "suffering disgrace for the Name," they were feeling no such pain at the time!

When the disciples were initially warned against speaking in the name of Jesus, the offense was over the proclamation of His *resurrection*. The Holy Spirit manifested Himself in the healing of the forty-year-old man who had never walked. So far, so good; no problem . . . yet. It was Peter's preaching about Jesus' resurrection that upset the Sadducees and got the apostles into trouble. This led the early Church to have a prayer meeting, praying for more power when preaching and to do miracles. The result was a very unusual manifestation of the Spirit—"The place where they were meeting was shaken"—but *also* a renewal of Pentecostal power—"They were all filled with the Holy Spirit and spoke the word of God boldly" (Acts 4:31).

† BASIS FOR RENEWAL

This renewal of power as demonstrated in Acts 4:31 is the proof that we should expect subsequent Holy Spirit manifestations. Had there been nothing like this after Pentecost, one might have to say that there is no possibility of a further outpouring of the Spirit. The fact that the same words are used twice—"filled with the Holy Spirit" (Acts 2:4; 4:31)—shows that the coming of the Spirit on the Day of Pentecost was not necessarily a one-time manifestation. The phenomena of the wind, fire and supernatural understanding of languages may or may not reappear, but the *filling* of the Holy Spirit certainly does. This is what opens the door for manifestations of the Holy Spirit, some of which may be repeated and some perhaps not. We only know of one occasion when people were struck dead for lying to the Spirit (Acts 5:1–11), a sobering manifestation, and one occasion when Peter's shadow led to people being healed (Acts 5:15).

One of the more striking things demonstrated by the people of faith in Hebrews 11 is that not a single one of them got to repeat what had been done before. Each had to be a pioneer—to do what had never been done. The one thing they had in common was that they did what they did *by faith*. It is this ingredient that we should be (but are often not) aware of with manifestations of the Spirit in our own time. When you hear of accounts of people laughing or falling down, the criticism often is, "Where do you find this in Scripture?" I respond that in Scripture we see people doing what is unprecedented—following the pattern of the people of faith in Hebrews 11. They lay the groundwork for all of us who would dare follow in their footsteps. I myself have had an ambition for a long time to follow in the steps of those described in Hebrews 11—if God would grant it. I believe that anyone who desires to succeed the people of faith in Hebrews

11 must be willing to do what has not been done before—and to accept the stigma that goes with it.

† OFFENDING THE MIND TO REVEAL THE HEART

If we can repeat what has gone before us we may ward off the critics a little bit, yes; but the stigma lies in having to see manifestations that are so odd or different that they really do put some off. I fancy that God the Father has a brainstorm with the Son and Spirit from time to time, with the agenda "What can we do next that will offend sophisticated people?" I do not, of course, think that the Trinity need a committee meeting, but I do think God loves to *offend the mind to reveal the heart*. It was His idea to choose "the foolish things of the world to shame the wise" (1 Corinthians 1:27).

There is a pattern in church history for God to do what nobody with power and influence at the time thinks is truly from Him. "Who dares despise the day [or way] of small things?" (Zechariah 4:10). Who took John Wycliffe or the Lollards seriously? How many in authority revered John Hus? Who took notice of Martin Luther's nailing the 95 theses to the door at the Wittenburg Church? When he stood before the hierarchy and said, "Here I stand. I can do no other. God help me. Amen," who in the established church believed he was led by the Holy Spirit?

Jonathan Edwards taught us that the task of every generation is to discover in which direction the Sovereign Redeemer is moving, then move in that direction. The problem is, we usually fail to see where God is at work until much later. Jacob said, "Surely the LORD is in this place, and I was not aware of it" (Genesis 28:16). I want to have the kind of relationship with God that means I see early on where He is—and where He is not.

The greatest offense in human history was God sending His Son to die on a cross. But what Pharisee, Sadducee or priest recognized God at work when His one and only Son was right there in front of their eyes? Had you walked into Jerusalem on Good Friday and said, "What is God doing in this Holy City today?" the reply would have been, "It's Passover. We are celebrating what God did through Moses thirteen hundred years ago—that is, if that Jesus of Nazareth outside the city wall would hurry up and die so we can get on with things." Nobody—nobody that "mattered"—had any sense that God was at work that day, that "God was reconciling the world to himself in Christ, not counting people's sins against them" (2 Corinthians 5:19).

When Stephen was being stoned and said, "Look . . . I see . . . the Son of Man standing at the right hand of God," it was so offensive that "they covered their ears and, yelling at the top of their voices, they all rushed at him, dragged him out of the city and began to stone him" (Acts 7:56–58). Had Stephen said that today I can well imagine some "sound" evangelical stepping in to say, "That is not biblical, you heretic. Don't you know that Jesus is *sitting*, not standing, at the right hand of God?"

† WHITEFIELD AND WESLEY

When George Whitefield left Anglican pulpits and took to the fields to preach the Gospel, his old friend from Oxford, John Wesley, criticized him and rebuked him. Not only that, there were the bizarre manifestations that occurred when Whitefield preached. People shrieked, cackled, barked like dogs, laughed, cried, shook and screamed. John Wesley criticized Whitefield for this, too, saying these manifestations were not entirely of the Holy Spirit. Whitefield agreed. Then stamp out what is false and of the flesh, said Wesley. Whitefield replied that if you try to eliminate what is false you will kill what is real, too, so you have to leave things alone. The funny thing is, Wesley eventually preached in the fields, too—and the exact same unwelcome manifestations of the Spirit happened when he preached!

When I invited Arthur Blessitt to Westminster Chapel, our more sophisticated members were upset. They said that he was absolutely fine for Speaker's Corner in Hyde Park, but not for Westminster Chapel. Just before Arthur spoke for the first time, he asked some questions about "when I give the invitation." I swallowed. "We don't do that here," I said to Arthur. "We don't?" he queried. Seeing the look on his face made me say, "Well, if you feel led, go ahead." He replied, "I can tell you right now that I do." He did—and it marked the beginning of a new era for Westminster Chapel. I thought I would die a thousand deaths the first time Arthur stepped into the pulpit. It was the largest crowd I had seen there. He read the verse about greeting one another with a holy kiss and wondered how many people out there would like a holy kiss right now? So he had everybody stand and greet one another with a holy kiss—before he even responded to my welcome and said he was glad to be there! But when he preached there was incredible power. He gave an invitation to that packed auditorium. With no pressure at all he simply asked anybody who wanted to receive Jesus Christ to stand up. Dozens did. It was a night of nights. But people asked, "Can't you sort him out? He does these things that offend. We like him when he only preaches the Gospel." I remembered the story of Whitefield and Wesley. It was the same principle at stake. I said, "If you try to change what you don't like about him you will adversely affect the way God has made him." I learned to let Arthur be Arthur.

Another amusing story. When he met Dr. Martyn Lloyd-Jones, the latter had only one piece of advice for Arthur: "Don't let anybody change you." As a result of having Arthur with us, and accepting the changes he suggested for us—giving an invitation, witnessing on the streets, singing choruses as well as hymns—I nearly got fired! Half the deacons turned against me, seeing the issue as a theological one. But the church sided with the other six deacons and dismissed the deacons who had accused me of heresy. One of those who opposed me later admitted that the issue was not theological but that the changes we made catapulted them out of their comfort zone. It was a hard time. So much so that I pretty much vowed not to do anything controversial again! But I did. I opened the door to the prophetic. This was a manifestation of the Holy Spirit utterly new to me. But I became exposed to a type of ministry I had not even thought about—that there would be those with a valid prophetic gift who were given to the church and would bless the church. We were definitely blessed by this kind of ministry. I have always been glad I became open to this. I go into some detail in my book *The Anointing* and also *In Pursuit of His Glory*.

† THE TORONTO BLESSING

I can remember the time and place when I first heard about the so-called Toronto Blessing. What I heard shook me rigid. I said it wasn't of God, but to be honest I just plain did not *want* it to be of God—people falling down uncontrollably and laughing their heads off. I find that sort of thing offensive. But I had a deep-seated fear that it just might be of God. When I came to terms with it and knew I had to accept it, it was the best decision I had made since inviting Arthur Blessitt to Westminster Chapel. It paved the way, though, for my introduction to the source of an even greater embarrassment—Rodney Howard-Browne.

† LOUISE'S HEALING

Colin Dye, minister of Kensington Temple, asked if I wanted to meet Rodney, who was holding meetings at Wembley Conference Center. Sure, I said, I would be glad to meet him. My friend Lyndon Bowring went with me to have breakfast with this man who is alleged to be the "father" of the Toronto Blessing, although Rodney was only 33. I had seen a video of him which was quite outrageous, and I never dreamed I would take him seriously. But after being with him for a few minutes I asked if he would come to my church on Saturday and pray for my wife Louise (there was no chance of getting her to go to one of his meetings). He agreed. Louise had been very unwell. She had two serious conditions. First, a cough that had begun three years before and which no doctor or hospital had been able to heal. It was awful. She spent six nights out of seven coughing, having to go into another room so that she did not wake me up. Second, she was in a serious depression, no doubt caused by the cough. The situation was so bad that I feared having to resign from the church and return to America.

It was Saturday morning, December 17, 1994. Louise had been up all night coughing and had slept in. I feared she would miss Rodney altogether and he was going out of his way to come into central London. But she woke up at 9:40 and said, "I want that man to pray for me." We arrived at my vestry ten minutes late, but there were Rodney and Adonica and their children—having been given a cup of tea. Louise and I came in. She sat in my chair, tired and feeling pretty desperate. There was no pre-conditioning, no hype, no singing—nothing. Rodney and Adonica stood next to her and prayed for about five minutes. Louise remembers seeing a tear that fell onto her blouse from Adonica's cheek. I only know that Louise was instantly healed of her cough in that moment. That was seventeen years ago. Six weeks later she flew to Florida to attend Rodney's camp meeting. It was there she recalls falling to the floor from the pew when Rodney prayed for her, then rolling back and forth. She admits she became a holy roller! What is more, when she returned to London the depression had lifted, too.

Jesus said that they who are faithful in what is least are faithful also in much (Luke 16:10, KJV). Had I not obeyed the promptings I was nervously having to accept regarding the Toronto Blessing and the happenings at London's Holy Trinity Brompton, I would never—ever—have accepted Rodney. I am so glad I did. But it has cost me: people distancing themselves from me, unkind things on the Internet and ugly letters. One person wrote to assure me that Louise's healing was purely psychosomatic. At least that is better than saying it is all of the devil—which some believe. The easiest way out is to say that Rodney, Toronto, laughter and falling down is of the devil; that way you can dismiss it. People—like myself—do not want to say it is of God; otherwise we need to get on board!

† RETIREMENT MINISTRY

When I made the decision to retire after 25 years at the chapel, I planned to spend the rest of my life as a recluse, fishing in the Florida Keys. But I was given a "word" as I pondered it that went something very like this: *Your ministry in America will be to charismatics.* Oh no, surely not! I want to reach evangelicals—I have what they need and I have the credentials for them. But it turned out that after returning to the USA the overwhelming number of invitations in the States and all over the world have been from charismatics. I like to think that Paul had a similar reaction when he was told he would have to minister to Gentiles; I am sure he would have preferred to reach his own people and his own kind. But no.

Part of my retirement has been spent preaching alongside Jack Taylor and Charles Carrin. The three of us have suggested a description for our combined ministry together—Word (that's me), Spirit (Jack), Power (Charles). Jack has been a Southern Baptist all his life; he was one of their leading authors and evangelists—preaching in the top churches. He has paid a high price because of the stigma of embracing the things of the Holy Spirit. Charles had been a Primitive Baptist (much the same as Strict Baptist in the UK) until he had a supernatural confrontation with God when ministering as a chaplain to a Spirit-filled prisoner in Atlanta. You will recall I said that when there is a high level of the Spirit's power around, the sense of embarrassment vanishes. The acute sense of the Spirit's power compensates so much that the embarrassment is welcomed, if not also fun! But when the Spirit wanes—which for some reason always happens—the embarrassment kicks in and we are challenged to the core of our being about whether the stigma is worth it or not. That is what one faces with the Gospel itself—and all that flows from obedience to it. But I can testify that the stigma, the embarrassment and the shame is worth it all. There is no substitute for the heartwarming knowledge that you are in God's will. In the words taken from a great English hymn:

> Go, labour on; 'tis not for nought;
> Thy earthly loss is heavenly gain;
> Men heed thee, love thee, praise thee not;
> The Master praises: what are men?
>
> — *Horatius Bonar, 1808–89*

Yes. What are men?

What is more, there will be no embarrassment in heaven. Or regrets.

14

EMBARRASSING TRUTHS

If you hold to my teaching, you are really my disciples. Then you will know the truth, and the truth will set you free.

— *John 8:31–32*

I suppose the reason we all jumped at Darwin's Origin of Species was because the idea of God interfered with our sexual mores.

— *Sir Julian Huxley, 1887–1975*

I have devoted a good portion of this book to the Gospel. But there are further truths that I wish to mention as well. In chapter 8, "Out on a Limb," I mentioned some views I myself hold (and would die for) but which have not become a part of the Church's orthodoxy. Although not all who read this book will fully accept the doctrines espoused in this chapter, I felt compelled to state what I believe the Church must uphold. I am sure you will agree on one thing: They are the sort of doctrines people can find offensive.

† CREATION

> By faith we understand that the universe was formed at God's command, so that what is seen was not made out of what was visible.
>
> — *Hebrews 11:3*

Every generation has its stigma, by which the believer's faith is tested. In the earliest Church it was the claim that Israel's Messiah is Jesus of Nazareth who is the God-man: man as though He were not God, God as though He were not man. The offense was increased by the teaching that Jesus fulfilled the Law on our behalf and that we are saved by trusting what He did instead of trusting in our own works. This teaching was renewed by the Reformers in the sixteenth century. One could show how the offense has shifted from generation to generation. Not that truths change, but not all teachings continue to be on the cutting edge of what offends the world.

If it is not cool to be a born-again Christian in our day, it only adds to the embarrassment to claim that God created the heavens and the earth as stated in Genesis. Although the Hebrew word *yom*—day—allows for some flexibility with regard to how long a day might be, it is still a stigma to uphold the idea of Creation. Most scientists scoff at it. But not all.

However, the main thing that I want to say in this chapter is that on matters of faith we must take our cue from Scripture, not from scientists. It worries me that Christians have listened to the latest word "science" says on the matter, then they turn to the Bible and try to make it fit.

Please note, *by faith we understand* that the universe was formed at God's command. The writer did not say "by science," "by observation" or "based upon evidence." We take our cue from the Word of God, however naïve that may seem.

I have a very high view of Scripture. I believe that holy men of old—both Old and New Testaments—wrote "as they were carried along by the Holy Spirit" (2 Peter 1:21). I believe that "all Scripture is God-breathed" (2 Timothy 3:16), that is, written by the Holy Spirit. Holy Scripture is a bit like the Incarnation. Jesus was man. Jesus was God. The Bible was written by man. The Bible was written by God. He used human personality and gifting and selected the men who wrote our Bible. But they wrote only what is true, putting down "true truth," as Francis Schaeffer would say. Take a close look at Hebrews 11:1: "Faith is being sure of what we hope for and certain of what we do not see" ("the conviction of things not seen," ESV). Faith to be *faith* is believing, or being convicted, without the evidence. "That is ridiculous," say the atheistic scientists. But that is why we are Christians and they are not. We believe *in* God and we also believe God. Faith is believing God. If you are controlled by the "evidence" and then turn to the Bible because you want to show some respect for it, you are being more influenced by the so-called evidence than you are by Scripture. In the case of today's consensus about evolution, many are persuaded by it but want to be good Christians, so they come up with a view of Creation that is not suggested by Scripture at all but by "science." The thing is, science is always changing. Read a book on science from fifty years ago. Much of what was once taught bears minimal resemblance to what is being taught today. Not only that, scientists are constantly changing their minds. The development of Darwinian theory means that what it is today looks quite different from what Darwin initially proposed.

The writer of Hebrews states that "what is seen was not made out of what was visible." The biblical position is creation *ex nihilo*—out of nothing. If there had been "something" before God spoke matter into existence, then the Genesis account got it wrong. Matter is not eternal. God created matter. This means there was not even a speck of dust in remotest space—only God. Had there been a speck of dust before God created the universe, then He made it with something already visible.

I would not be the slightest bit surprised to learn that scientists all over the world had suddenly seen the folly of evolution and affirmed a new view—even Creation. But would this make them Christians? No. Should we then believe Hebrews 11:3 because they disavow evolution? No. We should believe it anyway. We must *begin* with Scripture.

I am amazed that Sir Julian Huxley was so honest when he admitted why the world—in his opinion—welcomed Darwin. But at the bottom of the unbeliever's mind when they reject Creation as stated in Genesis is their lifestyle. They do not want to change the way they choose to live. Evolution confirms them in this decision; the thought of Creation horrifies them. It would mean there is a God to whom they must be accountable.

Do not be ashamed of the stigma of believing in Creation. One day God will vindicate His Word openly. Do not wait until then to be convinced. Believe it now—not by the external "proofs" of Scripture but by the internal testimony of the Holy Spirit. Those who believe on Him will not be ashamed.

† PREDESTINATION

> And those he predestined, he also called; those he called, he also justified; those he justified, he also glorified.
>
> — *Romans 8:30*

Predestination means that God makes choices before we do. It is His universe. When Jesus died for us, He bought us—like it or not, we are owned by Him (1 Corinthians 6:20).

I cannot answer all the questions that could come up from this chapter. I have some of my own. But I will say up front that, in my opinion, the absence of understanding of the sovereignty of God is one of the main reasons for the superficiality we see in today's Church. Oh dear. The idea of God being sovereign is not even on the radar screen of too many people who have a platform. It makes their God look so small.

God said to Moses, "I will have mercy on whom I will have mercy, and I will have compassion on whom I have compassion." Paul added his own interpretation of this word to Moses from Exodus 33:19: "It does not, therefore, depend on human desire or effort, but on God's mercy" (Romans 9:16). Romans 8:30—quoted above—says basically two things: (1) that the only people who are justified are those who were first called and that those who had been called—and only they—were predestined; and (2) that those who are predestined will be called, justified and glorified. This is a convincing verse for the teaching of once justified, always justified since those who are justified will be glorified.

Is it a sin not to believe in predestination? No. Is it a sin not to believe in eternal security? Almost. I say that because if you really believe we are saved apart from works, then the possibility of losing your salvation is only rendered feasible if something you *do* disenfranchises you from the family. Works win out at the end of the day, if you do not believe in Romans 8:30 literally. Why believe in predestination? First, check all the references to it in the Bible. Have you honestly done that? Please do not be afraid to examine exactly what Jesus taught. Predestination is in there, but without using what has become a scary word. For example, "No one knows the Son except the Father, and no one knows the Father except the Son and those to whom *the Son chooses* to reveal him" (Matthew 11:27, emphasis mine). These are Jesus' words and He admits to making the choice of who will know the Father. So, too, here: "For just as the Father raises the dead and gives them life, even so the Son gives life to whom *he is pleased to give it*" (John 5:21, emphasis mine). "*All those the Father gives me will come* to me, and whoever comes to me I will never drive away" (John 6:37, emphasis mine).

Luke made an editorial comment he did not have to make. Reporting that the Gentiles came to Christ in faith, he added, "And all who were appointed for eternal life believed" (Acts 13:48). The King James Version says, "As many as were ordained to eternal life believed." Luke might have said, "As many as believed were appointed to eternal life"—that would have been true! But he took a theological position: As many as were appointed to eternal life believed. The choice was made by God long before.

When I came to believe in this teaching—which happened in the days *immediately* following my meeting the Lord on October 31, 1955—it was without anybody's help. No Nazarene believed this. I knew no Baptists or Presbyterians. I did not know anybody who did believe what I discovered. I learned later that this was the teaching of the Church fathers like St. Augustine, medievalists like Thomas Aquinas, the Reformers (like Luther and Calvin), the Puritans (like John Cotton and John Bunyan), the hymn writers (like Isaac Watts, John Newton and Augustus Toplady), the evangelist George Whitefield, the theologian Jonathan Edwards and the preacher Charles H. Spurgeon. Mind you, all these men could be *wrong!* But it comforted me no end to find that what I discovered on my own from reading the Bible while a Nazarene was upheld, by and large, by the greatest people in church history. But even the denominations that have long held to this teaching are abandoning it. It is admittedly offensive. Because you will ask, "Why doesn't God choose everybody?" I have no idea. I wish He did. If He left it up to me, I would choose everybody and eliminate hell altogether. But I am called to uphold what I do not always understand and preach what I may not want to be true. I am convinced that in the words of an old song, "Someday He'll make it plain to me, someday when I His face shall see." Until then I will uphold what is not always very acceptable and let Him clear things up in His time.

The second reason for believing in predestination, as many testify, is that it will give you a deep, solid, settled and confident feeling that God is on the throne. It is a wonderful, wonderful feeling. For some it is no stigma at all. Although good people disagree on some of the aspects of this teaching, it is my own experience that many of those who have come into this understanding say that they notice this first of all—that God is so powerful and in control. Joni Earekson Tada, whose horrific diving accident left her paralyzed, told me that this teaching is what gave her a sense of sanity and purpose in life. It will increase your faith. Do not wait until you get to heaven to learn that God had His eye on you from before He created the world and that He is not going to let you go until you are safely in heaven. Do not wait until then! Believe it now!

† ETERNAL PUNISHMENT

Twice in recent years Louise and I have journeyed to Enfield, Connecticut, in order to pray and stand at the exact place where the most famous sermon in America was preached. It became one of the most memorable and pivotal moments in American church history, arguably the reason there is a Bible Belt in the United States to this day. On July 8, 1741, Jonathan Edwards took his text from Deuteronomy 32:35: "Their foot shall slide in due time." The printer gave it the title "Sinners in the Hands of an Angry God." The thesis of the sermon can be summed up as this: "There is nothing that keeps wicked men at any one moment out of hell, but the mere pleasure of God." Edwards depicted hell as real and never ending.

When I was in high school in Ashland, Kentucky, Edwards' sermon was required reading. The teacher quickly dismissed the contents of it to all of us and nobody took it seriously. But when it was actually preached the people in the church began to weep and moan loudly; the noise made Jonathan Edwards stop to urge the people to be quiet so he could continue. He read every word. When he finished, people were holding on to the pews of the church inside and strong men were holding on to tree trunks outside to keep from sliding into hell. The fact that Edwards preached the exact same sermon elsewhere with no effect whatsoever persuades me that it was the Holy Spirit who sovereignly owned the sermon when it was preached in Enfield. It took place at the height of America's Great Awakening.

This section of my book would probably get the prize for being the most difficult and offensive teaching in the Bible. I would define hell as a permanent state of conscious punishment for sin beyond the grave. Just remember, it's not an idea most people would have thought of. It's certainly not my idea. Ludwig Feuerbach (1804–72), the German philosopher who was the father of Marxism, argued that God is nothing more than a human projection upon the backdrop of the universe. His idea was that frail human beings need to believe there is a God "up there" who will look after them and reward them with heaven when they die—all this being our imagination. I reply: Given that presupposition, what human being would have come up with the idea of *hell?* It is the most horrible, unpleasant and painful destiny ever conceived. Who would have thought of it? It is God's idea. I wish it were not true.

It is Jesus who had more to say about hell than any other writer in the New Testament. It is either true, or it is not. If what Jesus taught is true it means that hell is even worse than Jonathan Edwards depicted it to be.

Five Possibilities

When you consider the destiny of unsaved people after they die, there are five possibilities: (1) atheism: people die like any animal; (2) universalism: all people are saved and no one is lost; (3) annihilationism: they cease to have any conscious existence whatsoever—as though they had never been born in the first place; (4) purgatory: some, perhaps all, eventually go to heaven after a period of time; and (5) conscious eternal punishment: they go to hell which has no end. I would hope that either universalism or annihilationism is true. If God asked me to decide, I would advise Him to save everybody.

The view that the unrepentant will be annihilated has been an attractive option for a surprising number of evangelicals in recent years. What was once taught only by the cults has now been embraced by some New Testament scholars, who use the combination of Greek philosophy and the Greek language to show that annihilation is what Jesus taught. For example, the Greek word *apollumi*—to destroy or perish—is the word used in John 3:16: "For God so loved the world that he gave his one and only Son that whoever believes in him shall not *perish* [they say it means soul and body annihilated], but have eternal life." Those who argue this—including some good friends of mine who are certainly not cult members or theological liberals—say that annihilation does not occur when they die but that they will have to stand before the Judgment—and then they will be destroyed. Apart from their interpretation of the Greek, they argue that immortality of the soul is not a creation gift but a regeneration gift. Only those who are converted, they say, are given immortality—a word that these scholars would use interchangeably with eternal life. They further argue that immortality of the soul—that all people (saved and lost) consciously exist after death—is Platonic and not Christian. I would point out that *apollumi* actually meant to destroy in the sense of wasting, as in the case of the perfume in the alabaster jar—"Why this waste [*apoleia*]?" (Matthew 26:8). This is not the same as annihilation. A modern equivalent might be when an insurance company regards a wrecked car as a write-off. The wreckage itself does not disappear.

The classical, old-fashioned view of heaven or hell—that the saved go to heaven and the lost go to hell—is what the Bible teaches. Summed up: "Then they will go away to eternal punishment, but the righteous to eternal life" (Matthew 25:46). You might also take a look at my treatment of the rich man and Lazarus (Luke 16:19–31) in my book *The Parables of Jesus*. I have barely touched this subject here but I could not leave it out. As for the Christian bearing a stigma, it does not get worse than this. But it is part of the Word of God to which we are bound by faith. Some say, "I believe in heaven but not in hell."

I answer that if there is no hell, then there is no heaven. Your only authority for believing in heaven is the Bible—which also teaches hell.

I predict that what seems unfair and wrong to us now will not seem that way then. When God clears His Name, we will all worship Him and admire Him more than ever. And when He explains other things to us—including the subjects of this chapter—at this, too, we will bow down and worship.

15

OUTSIDE
THE CAMP

*And so Jesus also suffered outside the city gate to make
the people holy through his own blood. Let us, then, go
to him outside the camp, bearing the disgrace he bore.
For here we do not have an enduring city, but we are
looking for the city that is to come.*

— Hebrews 13:12–14

*Now Moses used to take a tent and pitch it outside the
camp some distance away, calling it the "tent of meeting."
Anyone enquiring of the LORD would go to the tent of
meeting outside the camp.*

— Exodus 33:7

I was honored to speak at the Airport Vineyard Fellowship at Toronto in January 1996. The occasion was the second anniversary of the Toronto Blessing, although the "blessing" had not come on me. In January 1994 the Holy Spirit fell on that church in an extraordinary manner. By April people were going to that little church from all over the world, taking the blessing back to their own churches. The blessing eventually came to London's Holy Trinity Brompton Church. The news of it made the front pages of *The Times* and the *Daily Telegraph*. The *Sunday Telegraph* gave it the name "Toronto Blessing."

But the occasion of my speaking was no blessing for me. Without doubt it was the most frustrating, agonizing and embarrassing moment of my entire preaching career. I had wrestled for days about what to preach on. I could think of nothing. I wanted something new and fresh, but nothing gripped me. Seconds before Pastor John Arnott introduced me, I decided to resort to my old faithful "sugar stick" (every preacher has one)—my sermon on Hebrews 4:16, "Let us then approach God's throne of grace with confidence, so that we may receive mercy and find grace to help us in our time of need." I have preached that sermon what seems like thousands of times—certainly more than any other. I know it backward and forward. But when I proceeded to read the text I was hardly able to speak! I struggled to read the text, barely got through it, then began to introduce my old sermon: "The writer is addressing discouraged Christians . . ." I could not get any further. I tried again. "This passage refers to . . ." I could not say more. I prayed like I have not prayed in my life.

I tried again. "The epistle to the Hebrews . . ." I was unable to move beyond those words. I labored with all the strength of mind I could muster for the next ten minutes or more. I could not utter a single intelligible sentence. Four thousand people in front of me were laughing their heads off, my wife on the second row included. Lyndon Bowring was there, watching me struggle and having the time of his life! Not only was this moment no blessing, it was humiliating and terrifying. I could only think of the critics back in Britain, fearing what they would say since I am known as an expository preacher. They were astonished that I had endorsed this "blessing" and I knew they would say that I should be able to preach better than ever if this blessing was from the Holy Spirit!

If you had offered me a million dollars tax-free to preach that sermon I would not have been able to do it. I might just as easily have pushed a giant lorry up a hill with my bare hands. Approximately fifteen minutes later—praying like mad and in a panic in front of all these people and video cameras—a verse happily popped into my head but I could not recall what it said: Hebrews 13:13. I announced to the crowd, "Let's try a different text." They roared with more laughter. I turned to see what it said: "Let us, then, go to him outside the camp, bearing the disgrace he bore." I then read that verse aloud. The place got quiet. It would be an exaggeration to say you could hear a pin drop, but from that moment on I soared—I preached with liberty, ease and authority on going forward "without the camp" and "bearing the disgrace he bore." Several hundred responded to the invitation.

There is more to the story. I did not know it then, but I was the first person to preach in the "new" church! Yes. That church for some reason had been disenfranchised by the Vineyard Church, of which they had been a part for years, so they had to change their name. That very day was the first day it was called Airport Christian Fellowship. They had been forced to go forward "without the camp." I realized later that my sermon, as it turned out, was most appropriate for them. You may ask, "Why didn't the Holy Spirit give me that word before I started to preach in the first place?" You tell me. I can only surmise that, although I had not received the Toronto Blessing as others testify, I experienced *power* that night. A power that kept me from preaching a sermon I knew from memory and a power to preach on a text more relevant to those precious people than I could have dreamed.

† PROCEEDING OUTSIDE THE CAMP

Do you know what it is to proceed "outside the camp"? This is a reference to having to "go it alone," as opposed to having the institutional movement with you and behind you. For these Hebrew Christians—in a time of discouragement and non-vindication—the writer points out that Jesus Himself was crucified just outside the gate, or wall, of old Jerusalem. The city was too holy to allow a crucifixion—a Roman idea in any case—within its walls. So this sort of thing was outside the city.

It followed an ancient historic pattern, however. The reference to being "outside the camp" had two connotations—good and, perhaps, not so good. The most glorious occasion of being outside the camp was when Moses spoke to the LORD in what was called a Tent of Meeting. It was there that Moses spoke to the LORD "face to face." When Moses headed toward that tent, all the people rose and stood at the entrances to their tents, watching him. When Moses entered the tent, the "pillar of cloud would come down and stay at the entrance, while the LORD spoke with Moses" (Exodus 33:7–11). It was one of the most sublime, sacred and memorable times in ancient Old Testament history.

The "tent of meeting" was located outside the camp, that is, some distance away from where the people lived.

But there was another connotation as well. It pertained, for example, to the sin offering: "Then he shall take the bull outside the camp and burn it as he burned the first bull" (Leviticus 4:21). The "flesh and the hide he burned up outside the camp" (Leviticus 9:11). But there is more. A blasphemer's punishment was being stoned to death. Moses spoke to the Israelites and they took the blasphemer "outside the camp" (Leviticus 24:23). Not only that, a person with an infection was required to live "outside the camp" (Leviticus 13:46). When Miriam opposed Moses, she was afflicted with leprosy and was required to remain outside the camp (Numbers 12:15). Being outside the camp was a mark of disgrace and shame.

All the history contained above lay behind the admonition for Hebrew Christians to proceed and look to Jesus Christ "outside the camp." They would have applied this history to their present situation. It meant two things. First, they were identified with Jesus—our sin offering, our substitute and fulfillment of the Law—who was crucified outside the camp. But as Jesus was seen by the Jews as cursed and a blasphemer (Matthew 26:65–66), so would they be seen as walking in His steps. "Cursed is everyone who is hanged on a tree" (Galatians 3:13, ESV). Blasphemers were executed outside the camp. So, punishment for sin was carried out outside the camp. It all fit perfectly; they were to be totally identified with Jesus. It was bearing the stigma, the reproach, the disgrace. The writer exhorts them, "Don't be ashamed! Go for it!" he is saying to them. It was a privilege.

But there is more! The glory of the Lord is to be seen outside the camp. The fact was that the Tent of Meeting—where God spoke to Moses face-to-face—was outside the camp. If you want to speak to God face-to-face, do you desire this enough that you are willing to go outside the camp? This gives a fairly strong hint that if you want intimacy with God it may have to come not within the established religion but outside it. Moreover, the pillar of cloud—the glory of the Lord—was present outside the camp. It is therefore not an ominous or depressing lot but a glorious privilege to be outside the camp.

† THE RISE OF DENOMINATIONS

Nearly all denominations had their greatest blessing outside the camp; that is, they grew most and fastest outside the official institutional church. All the Reformers had this experience. The Puritans experienced it. John Wesley and George Whitefield did their greatest work outside the camp. The early Baptists were part of the Separatist Movement in England and were outside the camp. The Southern Baptist Convention, however, is now the biggest Protestant camp in the world. The Salvation Army was born outside the camp. Pentecostals started inside but eventually went outside the camp. Some charismatics started new churches, others stayed in the established church but "went outside the camp" in the way they approached things—and sometimes suffered for it. Early Nazarenes were born and thrived outside the camp.

The problem is, what is outside the camp today is the new camp tomorrow! The new camp always gets institutionalized. Martin Luther left Rome, but eventually there arose a Lutheran Church. John Calvin left Rome as well but from his school in Geneva came the Presbyterians. John Knox went to Geneva and got fired up and returned to his native Scotland. We have the Church of Scotland. But some went outside the camp and formed the Free Church of Scotland. It, too, became a new camp and some have left it to form a new church. The early Methodists left the Church of England. They began outside the camp but the Methodist Church became a huge—and respectable—camp. Indeed, the Salvation Army and the Nazarenes were virtually thrust out of the Methodist Church! The Cane Ridge Revival was outside everybody's camp, but when its leading light, Barton Stone, started the Christian Church from it, it became the new camp.

The principle, however, is this. The Tent of Meeting was temporary, so when we go outside the camp we may—for a while—experience a sense of the immediate and direct presence of God. And a touch of glory. But we will lose that as we become institutionalized and become the next camp. When someone figures out how to go outside the camp without becoming the next institutionalized camp, it will be unprecedented. Mind you, there will always be the loners and strange people of this world who never get along with anybody. I am not talking about them, but rather about those who, for strong spiritual reasons and convictions, need to move on from where they have been.

It is a great privilege to bear the disgrace of Christ. But remember that those who did so in the New Testament never ever had a sense of self-pity but rejoiced that they were counted worthy to suffer the disgrace of the Name (Acts 5:41). It is important to remember this. Sometimes those who are outside the camp can feel persecuted and, if they are not careful, become a bit self-righteous. Self-righteousness and self-pity are the twin sins we must avoid like the plague if we are found—at any time—outside the camp.

Is it so bad or wrong to be *inside* the camp? No. The Hebrew Christians had hoped to win all Jews—and thus stay within the circle of Judaism. It would have made one big glorious camp! But it was not meant to be. Jesus' parable of the tenants is about this issue. "I tell you," said Jesus, "that the kingdom of God will be taken away from you [the Jews] and given to a people who will produce its fruit." When the chief priests and the Pharisees heard this parable, "they knew he was talking about them" (Matthew 21:43, 45). But this did not take God by surprise. Hundreds of years earlier it was prophesied:

> I revealed myself to those who did not ask for me;
> I was found by those who did not seek me.
> To a nation that did not call on my name,
> I said, "Here am I, here am I."
> All day long I have held out my hands
> to an obstinate people,
> who walk in ways not good,
> pursing their own imaginations—
> a people who continually provoke me to my very face.

> — *Isaiah 65:1–3*

Isaiah had seen long ago that God's chosen people would reject His Son.

If one can stay within the camp—"in it to win it"—who is to say they are not led by the Holy Spirit? If a giant movement can maintain the anointing of the Holy Spirit—because they are open to the Word and the Spirit—wonderful! But I fear that this is rare. Therefore, when one is truly led outside the camp it should be a badge of honor. It means you are among those whom God is presently pleased with. He has revealed Himself to you! Thank Him for it. Welcome the stigma that comes with being forced to leave where you have been. And do not feel sorry for yourself or become self-righteous.

I know what it is to be outside the camp and then go back into it! One must be willing to go outside the camp. There is a time for this. But as it is true (count on it) that those outside the camp become the camp of tomorrow, so those outside the camp today may have to go back to yesterday's camp—and swallow their pride. Being "outside the camp" may be a temporary sojourn. The Tent of Meeting was an era of extreme blessedness. But it did not last forever. So if you are outside the camp at the moment, make an impact for God in that time. But remember that you will either be right in the middle of tomorrow's camp—and become the very thing you opposed today—or be required to tiptoe back into the camp you left!

There is one final thing I wish to mention. "For here we do not have an enduring city, but we are looking for the city that is to come" (Hebrews 13:14). Being outside the camp is not everything; being inside the camp is not everything. What matters is that we are on our way to heaven. Do not forget this! *We have no continuing city.* The camp itself is temporary. Being outside the camp is temporary. One thing is permanent—heaven. It is what kept Abraham going when he left his homeland. "For he was looking forward to the city with foundations, whose architect and builder is God" (Hebrews 11:10). Moses left the most prestigious camp of all—the palace of Pharaoh—because he saw "disgrace for the sake of Christ as of greater value than the treasures of Egypt" (Hebrews 11:26). All that he constructed and conceived—the Tabernacle and the sacrificial system—pointed to the death of Jesus Christ whose blood makes us fit for heaven.

As it is not cool to be a born-again Christian, neither is it "politically correct" nowadays to stress going to heaven rather than doing good for the world here below. But I know one thing: Church history will testify that those who did the most good on earth were those who were preparing people for heaven.

Here is a scenario that is repeated too often: First-generation missionaries go to save the lost; the unsought result is that those who come to Christ become movers and shakers and want to improve their way of living. So they are inspired to build roads and schools and hospitals. It all started because missionaries warned them of hell and promised them heaven if they would trust in the blood Jesus shed on the cross. But the second-generation missionaries—although no doubt largely because of things becoming institutionalized—often *only* go to build hospitals and schools and roads, and forget the lost. By the time you get to the third generation you have those who think about their homes abroad, their salaries and their security.

Whatever happened to the Gospel? This is the primary stigma. It is about Jesus dying to destroy death so that through the final resurrection we will be presented faultless before God. We are "looking for a city that is to come." Do not misunderstand me. I believe in doing all we can to improve things below. We must feed the poor. "Religion that God our Father accepts as pure and faultless is this: to look after orphans and widows in their distress and to keep oneself from being polluted by the world" (James 1:27). James 2:14, as we saw in a previous chapter, is totally about saving the poor man by good works. Oswald Chambers said that some people are so heavenly minded that they are of no earthly use. But why do we show the poor man that we care? Why reach out to people to improve their quality of living? So they can have a "good life" and go to hell? Do we need to be so coy about our motives? The stigma of the Gospel is that it has to do with fitting men and women for heaven. Have we forgotten this? Are we ashamed of it?

William Booth, founder of the Salvation Army, always said that it is hard to preach the Gospel to a person with an empty stomach. So they fed the poor. But why? Was it to send them on their way unconverted? No. They fed the poor in order to have an entry point to preach the Gospel to them! At the first graduation service of the Salvation Army, William Booth began his address with these words:

> Brothers and sisters, perhaps I should apologize to you that we have kept you here for these two years—all so that you could learn how to win a soul to Jesus Christ. It would have been better had you spent five minutes in hell.

Thank you for reading this book. I pray you will never be the same again. Do not be ashamed of the Gospel or the stigma that it carries. It is such an honor to be identified with the Son of God, our Creator and Redeemer.

May the blessing of God Almighty—Father, Son and Holy Spirit—rest on you at this moment and forever. Amen.

Dr. R. T. Kendall was born in Ashland, Kentucky, on July 13, 1935. He has been married to Louise for more than fifty years. They have two children, a son (Robert Tillman II, married to Annette) and a daughter (Melissa), and one grandson (Tobias Robert Stephen).

R. T. is a graduate of Trevecca Nazarene University (A.B.), Southern Baptist Theological Seminary (M.Div.), the University of Louisville (M.A.) and Oxford University (D.Phil.*Oxon.*). His doctoral thesis was published by Oxford University Press under the title *Calvin and English Calvinism to 1647*. He was awarded the D.D. by Trevecca Nazarene University in 2008.

Before he and his family went to England, R. T. pastored churches in Palmer, Tennessee; Carlisle, Ohio; Fort Lauderdale, Florida and Salem, Indiana. He was pastor of Calvary Baptist Church in Lower Heyford, Oxfordshire, England (paralleling his three years at Oxford). He became the minister of Westminster Chapel on February 1, 1977, and was there for exactly 25 years, succeeding G. Campbell Morgan and D. Martyn Lloyd-Jones. He retired on February 1, 2002. His 25 years at Westminster Chapel have been written up in his book *In Pursuit of His Glory*.

Shortly after Dr. Kendall's "retirement," he became involved in the Alexandria Peace Process, founded by Lord Carey, former archbishop of Canterbury, and Canon Andrew White, the archbishop's envoy to the Middle East. From this came a special relationship with the late Yasser Arafat, president of the Palestinian National Authority, and Rabbi David Rosen, Israel's most distinguished Orthodox Jewish rabbi. R. T. and David wrote a book together, *The Christian and the Pharisee*.

Dr. Kendall is the author of more than fifty books, including *Total Forgiveness, The Anointing, Sensitivity of the Spirit, The Parables of Jesus, God Meant It for Good* and *Did You Think to Pray?* He has an international ministry and spends his time preaching and writing. He and Louise currently live on Hickory Lake in Hendersonville, Tennessee, where he fishes occasionally.

More From R. T. Kendall!

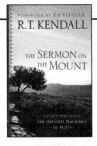